MACMILLAN MASTER GUIDES

General Editor: James Gibson

Published:

JANE AUSTEN: **PRIDE AND PREJUDICE** Raymond Wilson
     EMMA Norman Page
     MANSFIELD PARK Richard Wirdnam
ROBERT BOLT: **A MAN FOR ALL SEASONS**
EMILY BRONTË: **WUTHERING HEIGHTS** Hi
GEOFFREY CHAUCER: **THE PROLOGUE T**
     Nigel Thomas and
     THE MILLER'S TAL
CHARLES DICKENS: **BLEAK HOUSE** Dennis
     GREAT EXPECTATION
     HARD TIMES Norman P
GEORGE ELIOT: **MIDDLEMARCH** Graham Handley
    SILAS MARNER Graham Handley
E. M. FORSTER: **A PASSAGE TO INDIA** Hilda D. Spear
THE METAPHYSICAL POETS Joan van Emden
WILLIAM GOLDING: **LORD OF THE FLIES** Raymond Wilson
OLIVER GOLDSMITH: **SHE STOOPS TO CONQUER** Paul Ranger
THOMAS HARDY: **FAR FROM THE MADDING CROWD** Colin Temblett-Wood
    TESS OF THE D'URBERVILLES James Gibson
CHRISTOPHER MARLOWE: **DOCTOR FAUSTUS** David A. Male
ARTHUR MILLER: **THE CRUCIBLE** Leonard Smith
GEORGE ORWELL: **ANIMAL FARM** Jean Armstrong
WILLIAM SHAKESPEARE: **MACBETH** David Elloway
     A MIDSUMMER NIGHT'S DREAM Kenneth Pickering
     ROMEO AND JULIET Helen Morris
GEORGE BERNARD SHAW:
RICHARD SHERIDAN: **THE**
    THE

Forthcoming:

SAMUEL BECKETT: **WAITIN**
WILLIAM BLAKE: **SONGS O** **ERIENCE**
   A. Toml
GEORGE ELIOT: **THE MILL**
T. S. ELIOT: **MURDER IN TH**
HENRY FIELDING: **JOSEPH**
E. M. FORSTER: **HOWARD'S**
WILLIAM GOLDING: **THE SP**
THOMAS HARDY: **THE MAY** H. Evans
SELECTED POEMS OF GERALD MANLEY HOPKINS
PHILIP LARKIN: **THE WHITSUN WEDDING AND THE LESS DECEIVED**
   A. Swarbrick
D. H. LAWRENCE: **SONS AND LOVERS** R. Draper
HARPER LEE: **TO KILL A MOCKINGBIRD** Jean Armstrong
THOMAS MIDDLETON: **THE CHANGELING** A. Bromham
ARTHUR MILLER: **DEATH OF A SALESMAN** P. Spalding
WILLIAM SHAKESPEARE: **HAMLET** J. Brooks
     HENRY V P. Davison
     KING LEAR F. Casey
     JULIUS CAESAR David Elloway
     MEASURE FOR MEASURE M. Lilly
     OTHELLO Christopher Beddows
     RICHARD II C. Barber
     TWELFTH NIGHT Edward Leeson
     THE TEMPEST Kenneth Pickering
TWO PLAYS OF JOHN WEBSTER David A. Male

Also published by Macmillan

MASTERING ENGLISH LITERATURE R. Gill
MASTERING ENGLISH LANGUAGE S. H. Burton
MASTERING ENGLISH GRAMMAR S. H. Burton

WORK OUT SERIES

WORK OUT ENGLISH LANGUAGE ('O' level and GCSE) S. H. Burton
WORK OUT ENGLISH LITERATURE ('A' level) S. H. Burton

MACMILLAN MASTER GUIDES

BLEAK HOUSE

BY CHARLES DICKENS

DENNIS BUTTS

MACMILLAN

First edition 1986

Published by
MACMILLAN EDUCATION LTD
Houndmills, Basingstoke, Hampshire RG21 2XS
and London
Companies and representatives
throughout the world

Typeset by
TecSet Ltd, Sutton Surrey
Printed in Hong Kong

British Library Cataloguing in Publication Data
Butts, Dennis
Bleak House by Charles Dickens.—(Macmillan
master guides)
1. Dickens, Charles, *1812–1870*. Bleak House
I. Title II. Dickens, Charles, *1812–1870*
823'.8   PR4556
ISBN 0-333-40262-6 Pbk
ISBN 0-333-40263-4 Pbk export

CONTENTS

GENERAL EDITOR'S PREFACE

The aim of the Macmillan Master Guides is to help you to appreciate the book you are studying by providing information about it and by suggesting ways of reading and thinking about it which will lead to a fuller understanding. The section on the writer's life and background has been designed to illustrate those aspects of the writer's life which have influenced the work, and to place it in its personal and literary context. The summaries and critical commentary are of special importance in that each brief summary of the action is followed by an examination of the significant critical points. The space which might have been given to repetitive explanatory notes has been devoted to a detailed analysis of the kind of passage which might confront you in an examination. Literary criticism is concerned with both the broader aspects of the work being studied and with its detail. The ideas which meet us in reading a great work of literature, and their relevance to us today, are an essential part of our study, and our Guides look at the thought of their subject in some detail. But just as essential is the craft with which the writer has constructed his work of art, and this may be considered under several technical headings - characterisation, language, style and stagecraft, for example.

The authors of these Guides are all teachers and writers of wide experience, and they have chosen to write about books they admire and know well in the belief that they can communicate their admiration to you. But you yourself must read and know intimately the book you are studying. No one can do that for you. You should see this book as a lamp-post. Use it to shed light, not to lean against. If you know your text and know what it is saying about life, and how it says it, then you will enjoy it, and there is no better way of passing an examination in literature.

JAMES GIBSON

ACKNOWLEDGEMENTS

Cover illustration: *Doubtful Hope* by Frank Hull. © Forbes Magazine
Collection, New York, courtesy of Bridgeman Art Library.

1 CHARLES DICKENS: LIFE AND BACKGROUND

Charles Dickens was born on 7 February 1812 in Landport, a district of Portsmouth, where his father, John Dickens, worked as a clerk in the Navy Pay Office. In 1817 the family moved to Chatham, in Kent where Charles enjoyed a happy childhood around Rochester and in the surrounding riverside and country of the marshes.

Mr Dickens moved to work in London in 1822, but he was not very prudent financially and his fortunes declined so much that he was sent to prison for debt. What followed shattered young Charles. He was taken away from school and sent to work in Warren's Blacking Warehouse at Hungerford Stairs in London, and though the distressing experience only lasted a few months it left an indelible impression of shame and bitterness on the young boy's mind. The memory of feeling totally abandoned in the world was so powerful that Dickens could rarely bring himself to speak of it, even in later years when he was rich and famous.

A few months later Mr Dickens was discharged from prison and obtained work again, so he was able to rescue Charles from the Warehouse and send him back to school. As a boy Charles always read widely, particularly translations of *Don Quixote* and of *The Arabian Nights*, and such eighteenth-century novels as *Tom Jones* and *The Vicar of Wakefield*, and he also developed a lifelong interest in drama.

After leaving school at the age of fifteen in 1827 Dickens began work for Ellis and Blackmore, attorneys with offices in Gray's Inn, and he was soon occupied with getting wills registered and carrying legal documents to and from various lawyers. Because the pay was poor, Dickens soon moved to a post with Charles Molloy, a solicitor with offices in Symond's Inn, but finding this work dull he began to teach himself shorthand, and moved on again to become a law reporter in Doctors' Commons. All these experiences undoubtedly gave the young Dickens deep insights into the workings of the English legal system and the ways of lawyers and their clients which he was to think about and to use later.

After being a reporter of legal proceedings, Dickens became a newspaper reporter, often specialising in parliamentary reports, and he gradually built up a considerable reputation for the speed and excellence of his work. His attendance at parliamentary debates and political meetings sharpened his awareness of the social problems of the day: the poverty, the social unrest and all the difficulties occasioned by the Industrial Revolution which later led historians of this period to call it the Bleak Age. Dickens also began to doubt whether Parliament could ever deal with these problems in any satisfactory way.

At the same time as working as a reporter, Dickens also began writing short stories and sketches, mainly about the people and places of London, for various magazines and newspapers, and in 1836 a collection of these short pieces was published under a pseudonym as *Sketches by 'Boz'*. (Dickens had a younger brother nicknamed Moses and this became corrupted to 'Boses' and then 'Boz', the name Dickens eventually borrowed.)

One of the leading publishers of the day, Chapman and Hall, was so impressed by *Sketches by 'Boz'* that they commissioned its young author to write the letterpress to accompany a series of comic pictures dealing with a club of sporting characters which were to be drawn by a well-known artist, Robert Seymour. They were to appear in monthly instalments costing a shilling each, and the publishers thought they might sell as many as 400 copies a month. Under Dickens's dominant genius, however, the writing became more important than the illustrations, and when Seymour, who had been suffering from depression, committed suicide, he was replaced by a young illustrator Hablôt K. Browne, who used the pseudonym 'Phiz' to harmonise with Dickens's 'Boz'. Thus came about the successful partnership that made *The Posthumous Papers of the Pickwick Club* famous. The depiction of such comic characters as Mr Pickwick and his faithful servant Sam Weller, and such glorious scenes as Mr Pickwick's prosecution by the shady lawyers, Dodson and Fogg, helped raise the sales of the novel to about 40 000 a month, and set Dickens off on the start of a long career as England's most popular novelist.

Though *The Pickwick Papers* is mainly a comic novel, there are sombre episodes within it including several scenes set in prison. Dickens's next novel *Oliver Twist* (1837-9) concentrated more upon the harsher aspects of life with its powerful indictment of poverty and the treatment of the underprivileged in the early nineteenth century. *Nicholas Nickleby* (1838-9) exhibits both satire in its depiction of the ignorant schoolmaster Mr Squeers and compassion in its portrait of Smike, the abandoned schoolboy. *The Old Curiosity Shop* of 1840-1 was one of Dickens's greatest successes, and it seemed as if the whole country held its breath as it waited to see what would happen to the young heroine, in much the same way as followers of television serials today become involved in the lives of their characters. *Barnaby Rudge* (1841), the tale of riots in eighteenth-century London, followed, and in 1843 *A Christmas Carol*, with its depiction of Ebenezer Scrooge, the archetypal miser, proved one of the most popular of all Dicken's works.

By the 1840s he was the most successful writer in the English-speaking world. A married man with a growing family whom he loved to entertain with elaborate parties, he visited America in 1842 and later wrote a novel *Martin Chuzzlewit* (1843-4) incorporating some of his experiences there. A keen amateur actor, from the 1840s Dickens also began to appear regularly in productions of plays by such authors as Shakespeare and Ben Jonson, the public performances usually being given to raise money for charity. As if not busy enough with the writing of such novels as *David Copperfield* (1849-50), Dickens also found time to launch a new weekly magazine *Household Words* in 1850, which involved him in much editorial work, but even so the writing of his novels continued unabated.

The main reason for Dickens's great success as a writer seems to lie in his extraordinary ability to combine powerful, vivid and amusing story-telling with the capacity to make serious comments about life, especially its harsh economic realities, the cruelties of many Victorian legal and educational institutions, and the ways in which society's greed for money and the injustices of the class system blighted many lives, and did little to protect the poor and the deprived. In the early novels, such as *Pickwick Papers* and *Oliver Twist*, Dickens was not always able to integrate the diverse elements of his books into unified entities, but one of the most remarkable features of his wholly remarkable career is the way in which from the 1840s onwards he was with growing mastery able to combine popular and serious concerns, so that he could use comic characters and sensational incidents to make serious points.

As well as showing a greater control and unity, Dickens's novels from the 1850s also became more sombre in tone. The early novels, such as *Oliver Twist* and *Nicholas Nickleby*, were written at a time when conditions were appalling, and Dickens denounced them mercilessly. But there seems to have been a buoyancy, even an optimism, about those early books, as if Dickens believed that, though conditions were so dreadful, passionate denunciation would change them. Poverty, workhouses, bad schools could be abolished; society and the law could be reformed. Paradoxically, however, as material conditions began to improve for many people in the 1850s, Dickens's novels seemed to become less optimistic, as if he felt that an improvement in living conditions was not enough, and feared that the human spirit was in danger of being crushed by forces against which the individual had to struggle to retain any decent integrity.

Bleak House (1852-3) is such a superb example of Dickens's mastery of form and seriousness of meaning that many readers believe it is the greatest of all his novels. Its immediate origins are well known. After the final number of *David Copperfield* was published in October 1850, Dickens threw himself into amateur theatre work, which included several visits to Rockingham Castle in Northamptonshire, a house with a yew walk Dickens himself described as very like the Chesney Wold of the Dedlocks. Later in 1851 Dickens himself moved from his London home in Devonshire Terrace to a house in Tavistock Square, and he also took holidays on the English coast in 1852 and 1853, as well as staying in Boulogne, so it is not surprising that he had many thoughts of houses and residences in his mind during the writing of *Bleak House*, which he began in the autumn of 1851.

During this same period Dickens was also involved in discussions about housing conditions. In May 1851 he spoke to the Metropolitan Sanitary Association about the urgent need for sanitary reform, and later visited Bermondsey to inspect a possible site for new housing in January 1853, a visit that might well have supplied him with details for the description of the slum of Tom-all-Alone's which appeared in the fourteenth number of *Bleak House* (Chapter 46) published in April of that year. (*Tom-all-Alone's* was one of the possible titles Dickens had originally considered for the novel, along with *The Ruined House* and *The East Wind*, before he made his final decision.)

Contemporary political events also probably had some influence on the content of the novel, for when Lord John Russell resigned from the office of Prime Minister in February 1851 no one else could form a government for a fortnight, an event satirised in Chapter 40, which also seems to comment on the General Election of July 1852.

The most powerful influence behind *Bleak House*, however, is Dickens's passionate attack on the working of the Court of Chancery. This court, presided over by the Lord Chancellor, had been set up to provide help when the ordinary courts failed, and had developed into a system for settling disputes about legacies, trusts and disputed wills. But the slowness and ineffectiveness of its procedures were legendary. Dickens himself had gone to Chancery in 1844 to sue five publishers for breach of copyright, but although the Vice Chancellor ruled in his favour, the suit cost Dickens far more than any damages he was able to collect, and he complained that 'I was really treated as if I were the robber instead of the robbed.' Others fared even worse. The Jennings Case, begun in 1798, and the Day Case, begin in 1834, were still unsettled when Dickens began to write *Bleak House*. *The Times* newspaper attacked Chancery in 1851 and considerable public debate followed but, though reforms were introduced in 1852, there was still a good deal of dissatisfaction with the workings of the legal system, and further reforms followed in 1858, 1862 and 1873.

References to so many topical events (the story also includes a representative of the newly-formed Metropolitan Police branch of detectives as well as an example of the hardships endured by soldiers' wives - both subjects discussed in *Household Words*) might seem to suggest that Dickens was simply using them to add weight and realism to the more romantic events in the novel. What is so remarkable about so many of Dickens's later works, however, is the way in which he was able to weld so many apparently heterogeneous elements together, and use them to symbolise so much of what he felt was wrong not just with Victorian England but with the human condition in general.

When *Bleak House* began to appear in monthly parts in March 1852, it was a great popular success, selling even more copies than its predecessor *David Copperfield*, and it was followed by a series of works which continued to explore the 'Condition of England', including *Hard Times*, a devastating critique of utilitarianism, in 1854, *Little Dorrit* in 1855-7 and *A Tale of Two Cities*, a story about the French Revolution, in 1859.

From 1853, furthermore, Dickens had occasionally given public readings from his novels to raise money for charity, and in 1858 he began a series of readings which exceeded 400 by the end of his life. A superb mimic, he attracted huge audiences to his readings of comic scenes such as the trial of Mr Pickwick, or pathetic ones such as the death of Paul from *Dombey and Son* (1846-8). His reading of the brutal murder of Nancy by Bill Sikes in *Oliver Twist* was particularly sensational and absolutely shattered his audiences.

During the writing of *Bleak House*, however, Dickens began to complain of feeling overworked for the very first time in his life, and the breakdown of his marriage in 1858, involvement in a rail accident in 1865, and the strains of an immensely successful reading tour of America in 1867-8 gradually undermined his health. Despite the great success of *Great Expectations* in 1861 Dickens only finished one more full length novel, *Our Mutual Friend* in 1864-5, and he collapsed and died on 9 June 1870, while working on his last novel *The Mystery of Edwin Drood*. Though Dickens had hoped for a quiet burial in Kent, his body was laid to rest in Westminster Abbey, the particular resting place for English literary genius.

2 SUMMARIES AND CRITICAL COMMENTARY

2.1 OVERALL SUMMARY OF THE PLOT

Bleak House has a very complicated plot and the novel often switches from one apparently unrelated part to another. As the story proceeds, however, the connections between the different parts become clearer, and they are all seen to be related to each other. Some readers may find it initially helpful to think of the novel as consisting of two main stories – the *Chancery plot* of Esther, Ada, Richard and Mr Jarndyce, and the *Dedlock plot* of Chesney Wold, consisting of Sir Leicester and Lady Dedlock, and the activities of their lawyer Mr Tulkinghorn – but even these two major narrative threads are eventually seen to be part of the same story, as the following summary indicates.

In a nineteenth-century London so filled with fog that it even penetrates into the High Court of Chancery, the Lord Chancellor, who is presiding over the longstanding case of *Jarndyce* and *Jarndyce*, arranges for two young wards, Ada Clare and Richard Carstone, to be placed under the care of their older cousin, John Jarndyce.

Meanwhile, elsewhere in London in her town house, Lady Dedlock, wife of Sir Leicester Dedlock of Chesney Wold, Lincolnshire, and one of the claimants in the Jarndyce case, is startled when she sees the handwriting on a legal document brought by Mr Tulkinghorn, her husband's lawyer.

Mr Jarndyce appoints Esther Summerson as companion to his young wards. Before moving to his home, Bleak House, near St Albans, the young people spend the night with Mrs Jellyby, a lady who devotes all her attention to the cause of helping Africans and neglects her family. They also meet eccentric, old Miss Flite, another suitor in the Court of Chancery, and Krook, an illiterate rag and bottle merchant, who collects old legal papers in his dirty warehouse.

Illegitimate and not knowing anything about her parents, Esther had been brought up by her stern godmother, Miss Barbary, and Miss Barbary's servant, Mrs Rachel. After her godmother's death Ester was educated at Mr Jarndyce's expense and then invited to join him. She finds Bleak House very comfortable, and settles in happily with Mr Jarndyce and her two companions. Always looking for ways of doing good, one day she helps some poor brickmakers and their wives, when the philanthropic Mrs Pardiggle's insensitive behaviour fails to bring them any comfort.

Meanwhile Mr Guppy, the legal clerk whom Esther met in London, visits Lady Dedlock's house in Lincolnshire, and seems to recognise Lady Dedlock's portrait. Mr Tulkinghorn makes inquiries of Mr Snagsby, a law-stationer, about the identity of the writer of the legal document which startled Lady Dedlock. He discovers that the writer's name is Nemo, and that he lodges in Krook's Warehouse, but when he visits the dirty lodgings he finds that Nemo is dead. No one seems to know anything about Nemo except Jo, a poor, young crossing-sweeper, whom Nemo had befriended, and who now sweeps the step outside the cemetery where Nemo is buried. Lady Dedlock pretends to be indifferent to Mr Tulkinghorn's news.

Esther realises that Richard and Ada are gradually falling in love. After some indecision Richard decides to become a surgeon and moves to London, where Esther and Ada visit him and meet again Caddy Jellyby, now engaged to Prince Turveydrop, a dance-instructor. Esther also meets Allan Woodcourt, a young doctor, and helps the three Neckett children when Jarndyce's friend, Harold Skimpole, tells of their father's death. Richard gives up Medicine and begins to study Law instead, partly because he expects to profit from the Jarndyce case.

A veiled lady meanwhile visits Jo, who has wretched lodgings in Tom-all-Alone's, and asks to be shown the places where Nemo lived and is buried, and Mr Guppy becomes intrigued by the news. His friend Bart Smallweed's grandfather advises a debtor, Trooper George, that he could have made money if he had helped to find the missing Captain Hawdon. Mr Tulkinghorn pursues the mystery of the veiled lady, too, and Jo confuses her with Lady Dedlock's maid, Hortense.

Richard now decides to make his career in the army, but he and Mr Jarndyce quarrel over his engagement to Ada. Guppy introduces Esther to his friend Mrs Chadband, and Esther recognises her as Mrs Rachel, her godmother's servant.

Both Tulkinghorn and Grandfather Smallweed try to obtain examples of Captain Hawdon's handwriting from Trooper George, but he refuses to co-operate. Guppy tells Lady Dedlock of the resemblance he has noticed between her and Esther. He also reveals that, through meeting Mrs Chadband, he has discovered that Esther's real name is Esther Hawdon, and suggests that Lady Dedlock knew her father.

Esther herself, meanwhile, falls ill after trying to help the sick crossing-sweeper, Jo, and then nursing her own maid, Charley Neckett, back to health. Esther is blind for a time and much disfigured by her illness.

Guppy and his friend Jobling (under the name of Weevle) scheme to obtain Hawdon's letters from Krook, but he dies of spontaneous combustion and the papers disappear. The Smallweeds and Tulkinghorn finally succeed, however, in persuading Trooper George to hand over one of Hawdon's letters to Tulkinghorn.

Esther convalesces at the home of Mr Jarndyce's friend, Boythorn, in Lincolnshire, and there she meets Lady Dedlock, who confesses that she is Esther's mother, and believed that Esther had died at birth. Both women agree to keep the secret from Sir Leicester Dedlock and never to meet again.

Richard has now become deeply involved in the outcome of the Chancery case of Jarndyce and Jarndyce, and breaks with his guardian, suspecting him of being an interested party. Esther urges Mr Guppy to desist from making further inquiries about her and turns down his proposal of marriage. Richard's new legal adviser, Mr Vholes, entangles him further in debt.

Tulkinghorn now reveals to Lady Dedlock that he knows of her secret past, of her affair with an army captain, and of the child she gave birth to, though they were not married. He urges her to do nothing until he has decided what action to take, leaving Lady Dedlock in an agony of suspense. Snagsby complains that Lady Dedlock's ex-maid Hortense is pestering him, and she asks Tulkinghorn to find her a new post, but the lawyer threatens her with prison if she continues to be a nuisance.

Esther and Mr Jarndyce urge Skimpole to stop taking money from Richard, but Esther is startled when Sir Leicester visits Bleak House, and she decides to tell her guardian of her mother's identity. Mr Jarndyce reassures her, and asks her to marry him. Though she regrets the loss of Allan Woodcourt, Esther agrees.

Richard leaves the army, and Allan Woodcourt returns to England from his post as a naval surgeon. He meets Esther again and also befriends Jo, nursing him until his death. Richard's involvement with the Jarndyce case has become so obsessive that it makes him ill, and Ada discloses that they are already married, and moves into his lodgings near Chancery Lane.

Lady Dedlock dismisses her maid Rosa and, as a result, Tulkinghorn announces that he now feels free to expose her disgrace. After he leaves, Lady Dedlock also goes out. That night a gunshot is heard and next morning Tulkinghorn is found murdered.

Detective Bucket arrests Trooper George for the murder, and, when he refuses to ask for legal help, his friend Mrs Bagnet brings back his mother, Mrs Rouncewell, the housekeeper at Chesney Wold, to make him change his mind. Bucket reveals that Hortense was the murderess, however. When Lady Dedlock realises that her secret history is known, she writes her husband a farewell note, and then, veiling herself, leaves the house.

Sir Leicester suffers a stroke but summons Bucket to search for his wife, and offers his full forgiveness. Accompanied by Esther, the detective searches London without success and then takes a carriage to St Albans. He interrogates the brickmakers and learns that one of their wives has gone to London but that a veiled lady has gone north. After pursuing her for some time, Bucket suddenly turns round and returns to London. He explains to Esther that the two women have changed clothes, and Esther finds her mother lying dead on the step outside the cemetery where Captain Hawdon was buried.

Mr Jarndyce finds employment for Allan Woodcourt in Yorkshire and also gives him a cottage designed in the style of Bleak House. He now releases Esther from her engagement to him, and she and Allan plan to marry.

Grandfather Smallweed now produces a document which appears to be a will of later date than any other known in the Jarndyce case, but when Allan and Esther hurry to Court they find that the case is already over. The whole estate has been absorbed in its legal costs!

The disappointment devastates Richard, who dies begging Ada's forgiveness for the wrongs he did her. Chesney Wold falls silent, though Sir Leicester still visits his dead wife's mausoleum accompanied by his faithful servant Trooper George. Mr Jarndyce looks after Ada and her baby boy, and Esther and Allan live in modest contentment.

2.2 CHAPTER SUMMARIES AND CRITICAL COMMENTARY

Chapter 1

Summary

One foggy November afternoon, the Lord High Chancellor presides over the High Court of Chancery in Lincoln's Inn Hall, London. He is hearing legal arguments in the case of *Jarndyce* and *Jarndyce*, and when the hearing is adjourned, he arranges to meet a young girl and boy to discuss their going to reside with their cousin. A little old mad woman and a man from Shropshire are among unsuccessful suitors also present in the court.

Commentary

The opening paragraphs powerfully evoke the murky gloom of a dismal November afternoon, Dickens mainly achieving his effects by the repetition of such key-words as 'mud' and 'fog', the latter used no fewer than thirteen times in the second paragraph alone. The case of *Jarndyce* and *Jarndyce*, which is being heard in Chancery, seems to be a dispute about a will, but the legal system has been incapable of dealing with it swiftly and justly, so that the case has become a joke among lawyers, though a case of frustration and distress for many years to the people who expect to benefit from the settlement. Thus the literal mud and fog of the opening paragraphs are used by Dickens to symbolise the confusion and misery caused by the Court of Chancery and the case of *Jarndyce* and *Jarndyce*, for, as Dickens says, 'in the midst of the mud and at the heart of the fog, sits the Lord High Chancellor.' Nearly everyone in *Bleak House* is involved in the case in some way or other, and so doomed to the same foglike confusion and misery. At the purely narrative level Dickens raises the reader's curiosity about the identities of the young girl and boy, soon to be revealed as Ada and Richard.

Chapter 2

Summary
On that same November afternoon Sir Leicester and Lady Dedlock, visiting London from their home in Lincolnshire, discuss their part in the case of *Jarndyce* and *Jarndyce* with their lawyer, Mr Tulkinghorn. Lady Dedlock is startled by the handwriting she sees on one of Tulkinghorn's legal documents, and feels so faint that she leaves the room.

Commentary
Having introduced one setting and one group of characters in the first chapter, Dickens now switches his narration to the Dedlocks and the world of fashion in the next. The reader discovers that they too are involved in the world of Chancery and hence of its fog and mud. Indeed the description of the very wet Lincolnshire from which the Dedlocks have just come helps to make the connection between them and Chancery clearer. The Dedlocks, as their name implies, are locked out of life (or spiritually dead) in some way. Lady Dedlock might be bored because she has no children, Dickens seems to hint, but the reason for her lifelessness is really because she lost the child she once had, we discover later. The character of Mr Tulkinghorn is introduced very enigmatically.

Chapter 3

Summary
Esther Summerson describes how she was brought up very strictly by her godmother, Miss Barbary, who told her that her mother had behaved disgracefully and that she ought to forget her. After her godmother's death, Esther discovered that Miss Barbary was really her aunt, and a lawyer, Mr Kenge, told her that a Mr Jarndyce had offered to be responsible

for her education. She spent six happy years at Greenleaf School, and then Mr Jarndyce invited her to become companion to his ward of the Court of Chancery. In London, Esther meets Ada Clare and Richard Carstone, and the Lord Chancellor arranges for them to be placed under the care of Mr Jarndyce of Bleak House, with Esther as Ada's companion. As they leave the court, a little old mad woman, who is also awaiting a legal judgement, and is later identified as Miss Flite, greets them.

Commentary

A new character, Esther Summerson, is introduced, who is not only to become the novel's major heroine, but also the narrator of much of the story that follows. (Thus her method of telling the story in the first-person is a deliberate contrast to the way Dickens tells other parts of the story as an omniscient author, an aspect of narrative technique discussed in fuller detail in Section 4.2.) Esther's connection with the other events that have happened in the story becomes clearer when we realise that she is to become the companion to the two wards of Chancery who were introduced without their names at the end of the first chapter. Thus, in the three opening chapters of the novel, we have been introduced to three different groups and worlds - Richard and Ada, the Dedlocks, and now Esther, as well as such minor figures as the old mad woman and various lawyers. All these characters were introduced separately, but all have been revealed to have connections with each other. Dickens is beginning to depict a world in which human beings are mutually interdependent, but in which fog and confusion and injustice separate and frustrate them.

Those readers who criticise Esther for being excessively modest and unbelievably good later may find some clues to her character in the account of her painful upbringing; her adult behaviour can often be seen to derive from the lack of love and praise in her early years.

Chapter 4

Summary

Mr Kenge's clerk, Guppy, takes Ada, Esther and Richard to spend the night at Mrs Jellyby's house before they travel on to Mr Jarndyce's. Mrs Jellyby is a philanthropist who busies herself so much with correspondence about the settlement of Borrioboola-Gha in Africa that she neglects her family at home. Her children are in distress, her house dirty and the meal poor. Esther comforts the children and helps tidy up, but Mrs Jellyby's daughter, Caddy, breaks down and says the whole house is disgraceful and she wishes she were dead.

Commentary

The picture of dirt and chaos at Mrs Jellyby's parallels the darkness of

London and the Law in previous chapters, for each reveals a lack of order and responsibility. Chancery, the Dedlocks, and now Mrs Jellyby all display an unfeeling indifference, and Mrs Jellyby's drawing-room fire smokes unpleasantly just like the London fog. Dickens satirises Mrs Jellyby not for her philanthropic work – he was a tireless philanthropist himself – but for neglecting her family. One of the interesting contrasts in the novel is between those characters who can see clearly and those who fail to do so; and Mrs Jellyby's preoccupation with Africa rather than seeing what needs to be done at home leads Dickens to give this chapter its ironical title 'Telescopic Philanthropy'. Mrs Jellyby can only see problems a long way away, and it is no coincidence that one of her children is called Peepy.

Chapter 5

Summary

Next morning Esther, Caddy, Ada and Richard go for a walk and meet the little, old, mad woman encountered the previous day (later identified as Miss Flite). She insists on taking them to her lodgings in a squalid rag and bottle warehouse belonging to Mr Krook. Krook reveals that Barbary, Clare and Dedlock are also involved in the Jarndyce case, and he describes how Tom Jarndyce killed himself in despair at the case ever being settled. The old woman is obsessed with winning her own legal case, and keeps a number of birds in her room which she plans to release when judgement is given. At one o'clock a carriage arrives at Mrs Jellyby's to take Ada, Esther and Richard to Mr Jarndyce.

Commentary

While this chapter re-emphasises the chaos at Mrs Jellyby's, Dickens now introduces another area of muddle and neglect in Mr Krook's business. His shop is full of dirt and decay, and he is ironically known as the Lord Chancellor because 'we both grub on in a muddle'. The interdependence of all the characters is indicated again when Krook reveals that Barbary, Clare and the Dedlocks are also involved in the Jarndyce case. Krook's inability to read is to have important consequences in the plot later, and another irony of this chapter is that Esther passes the room where her unknown father is living. Miss Flite's birds, prevented from flying by their captivity, are powerful symbols of the way Chancery thwarts human happiness. (There is a fuller account of this chapter in Section 5.1 and 5.2).

Chapter 6

Summary

Esther, Ada and Richard travel through the countryside to Mr Jarndyce's home, Bleak House, which is near St Albans. Their host greets them warmly, though he complains of the east wind when he hears how Mrs Jellyby's children are neglected. He introduces another guest, Harold Skimpole, an apparently innocent, child-like creature with so little aptitude for business that his friends have to support him. During an evening when Esther realises that Richard and Ada are falling in love, Skimpole is arrested for debt. Esther and Richard pay the debt-collector from Coavinses and Skimpole is released, but Esther cannot help feeling that it is as if she and Richard had been arrested. Mr Jarndyce warns them never to pay Skimpole's debts again.

Commentary

Mr Jarndyce is embarrassed by expressions of gratitude, as his note to Esther shows, and he conceals his disappointment at the way people behave by complaining of a cold east wind. His generous personality represents the selfless practical philanthropy Dickens prefers to institutional bureaucracy. Skimpole, on the other hand, professes an ignorance of money which his enjoyment of the good things of life and dependence on the support of others, contradicts. Significantly, Mr Jarndyce says, 'You can't make him responsible', and entrusts Esther with the keys of the house, a symbol of responsibility.

Chapter 7

Summary

Meanwhile at Chesney Wold in Lincolnshire the wet weather continues. Mrs Rouncewell, the housekeeper, welcomes her grandson, Watt, who seems very interested in a pretty maid, Rosa. Two London lawyers ask permission to look around the house, and one of them, Mr Guppy, seems to recognise the portrait of the present Lady Dedlock, though he has never met her. After the lawyers have gone, Mrs Rouncewell tells Watt and Rosa about the terrace known as the Ghost's Walk, which is supposed to be haunted by the steps of an earlier Lady Dedlock when sickness or disgrace threatens the family.

Commentary

This chapter is full of dramatic clues to future developments, from the reference to Mrs Rouncewell's having two sons, one of whom 'went for a soldier', to the legend of the Ghost's Walk, which presages some impending disaster. Guppy has never seen Lady Dedlock but did meet somebody very like her at the beginning of Chapter 4! Guppy's feeling that he has seen Lady Dedlock before, though he knows this is unlikely, is an example of the *déjà vu* feeling many people have when they feel they have seen something or been somewhere before, although they know this is unlikely. In Guppy's case there is a logical explanation.

What is also very interesting, however, is the way Dickens gives the reader a *déjà vu* feeling here by introducing a character, Guppy, into the third-person narrative whom the reader has already met in the first-person narrative. This is a technique Dickens frequently used in *Bleak House*, asking us to see characters or places in a new light, and it is one of the principal ways by which he dwells upon 'the romantic side of familiar things' in the novel.

Chapter 8

Summary
Esther enjoys the order and comfort of Bleak House. Mr Jarndyce talks to her about the Chancery dispute, which initially concerned a will, but is now about obtaining legal costs. His great uncle, Tom Jarndyce, changed the name of the house from The Peaks to Bleak House because of the misery the case caused him. Mr Jarndyce praises Esther's wisdom and asks her to discuss Richard's career with him. One of his acquaintances, Mrs Pardiggle, another busy philanthropist, invites Esther and Ada to visit some poor brickmakers, and on the way Esther discovers Mrs Pardiggle's children are extremely unhappy at the way their mother treats them. Mrs Pardiggle's insensitive behaviour antagonises the brickmakers, but Esther and Ada offer sympathy and practical comfort to Jenny, a brickmaker's wife, whose baby has just died.

Commentary
The tragedy of the brickmakers dominates this chapter. The insensitive attempt at preaching by Mrs Pardiggle is completely ineffective and she reminds the reader of Mrs Jellyby and her unhappy children. Though Esther and Ada feel an iron barrier between the brickmakers and themselves, it is their practical benevolence which brings relief, as well as the moving humanity of the other brickmaker's wife. Esther's surprise at Mr Jarndyce's trust in her is a natural response to the way her self-confidence was destroyed in childhood. The discussion of Richard's career, just after the sad story of Tom Jarndyce, and the mention of Esther's handkerchief, hint at future developments.

Chapter 9

Summary
Ada and Richard gradually fall in love, but Richard's relative, Sir Leicester Dedlock, is unable to help his career. Mr Jarndyce's friend, Boythorn, who

is involved in a legal dispute with Sir Leicester over a question of alleged trespass, comes to stay. When the legal clerk Guppy visits him, Esther notices that he is much smarter than when they first met, and he proposes to her. Though she declines his offer, Esther is both amused and touched by it.

Commentary

The web of relationships which connects most characters in the novel continues to be revealed. Richard is related to Sir Leicester; Sir Leicester is in dispute with Boythorn; Boythorn's clerk is Mr Guppy; Guppy, who scrutinises Esther in an unusual way, proposes to her in comically extravagant language. Guppy's language and Boythorn's extremist personality give this chapter its humour, but in showing how characters are interconnected Dickens is making a serious point about society.

Chapter 10

Summary

Mr Tulkinghorn, Sir Leicester Dedlock's lawyer, leaves his home in Lincoln's Inn Fields, and visits Mr Snagsby, the law-stationer in Cook's Court, Cursitor Street. He wants to know who copied some affidavits used in the case of *Jarndyce* and *Jarndyce*. Snagsby's records give the name of the law-writer as Nemo, and Snagsby directs Tulkinghorn to Nemo's lodgings in Krook's rag and bottle shop. Tulkinghorn enters Nemo's foul and dirty room to find Nemo lying motionless on his bed.

Commentary

Tulkinghorn's attempt to discover who copied some legal documents is not really explained by Dickens, and the reader has to work out, therefore, that he is trying to discover the identity of the law-writer whose writing startled Lady Dedlock. (The reader has to become a detective, in other words.) Mr Tulkinghorn's character is mysterious, like his house, and the painting on the ceiling of Allegory, usually with a pointing finger suggesting lessons to be learned, is to become a recurring image in the novel. The Snagsbys, on the other hand, represent one of the many marriages in the novel which Dickens compares with each other, treating this one satirically. Nemo's identity is one of the novel's great mysteries.

Chapter 11

Summary

Tulkinghorn and Krook discover that Nemo is dead, and a young surgeon reveals that he died from an overdose of opium. No clue as to Nemo's identity is apparently found in his room, though the surgeon thinks he may once have been prosperous. Mr Snagsby is unable to provide any more information about him except that he came to the area eighteen months earlier and asked for work because he was hard up. At the inquest next day, the Coroner discovers that Nemo did have one friend, a crossing-sweeper named Jo, and he reveals that Nemo befriended him out of mutual loneliness, and occasionally gave him money. A verdict of accidental death is recorded and Nemo is buried in an ugly, evil-smelling cemetery. When night falls, Jo sweeps the step outside its iron gate.

Commentary

In describing the squalor of Nemo's death and burial-ground, and in revealing Jo's poverty and ignorance, Dickens is indicting Victorian society for its irresponsibility towards the less fortunate, his great theme in the novel. Dickens also develops his narrative by introducing two new characters, Jo and the surgeon, who are to become important later. Both Krook and Tulkinghorn have an interest in Nemo's portmanteau.

Chapter 12

Summary

Sir Leicester and Lady Dedlock return home from France, and Lady Dedlock praises the new maid, Rosa, to the annoyance of her own maid, Hortense. In January, Chesney Wold is full of fashionable guests, among them the politicians Lord Boodle and William Buffy, MP. Mr Tulkinghorn tells Lady Dedlock that the writer of the legal document she recognised is dead and that no one knew his name.

Commentary

Lady Dedlock's boredom and weariness continue, but she is obviously very interested in the identity of the dead law-writer, though she tries to conceal this from her husband and Tulkinghorn. Dickens satirises the politicians and their irresponsibilities by exposing the conceit of Boodle and Buffy, who behave as if only their followers and their families matter. The reference to Boythorn reminds the reader of the connection between Bleak House and Chesney Wold, and the jealousy of Hortense sows the seeds for other developments.

Chapter 13

Summary

After some indecision, Richard decides to become a surgeon, and he, Ada, Esther and Mr Jarndyce dine with lawyer Kenge's cousin, Mr Bayham Badger, who is to superintend Richard's medical studies. Mr Bayham Badger seems extraordinarily proud of the fact that his wife has had two previous husbands, and they spend most of the evening discussing them! Later Ada tells Esther that she and Richard are in love with each other, and Mr Jarndyce urges Richard to rely on his own efforts to win success for her.

Commentary

Worries about Richard's character clearly emerge in this chapter. Jarndyce suspects that his relying on the Chancery settlement has made him indecisive, while Esther believes that his public-school education is responsible. The comic account of Mrs Bayham Badger's three marriages contrasts with the love of Richard and Ada, and the references to Guppy and the dark, young surgeon suggest other love-affairs which the novel is going to examine. In reintroducing Allan Woodcourt, the doctor first mentioned in the *third-person* narrative of Chapter 11, Dickens uses the device of repetition so as to give another *déjà vu* effect.

Chapter 14

Summary

Richard begins his new career, and Mr Jarndyce, Esther and Ada visit London, where Caddy Jellyby tells them she is engaged to Prince Turveydrop, a dance-instructor. They visit the dance academy and meet Prince and his father, old Mr Turveydrop, who is celebrated for his deportment, but does not actually do any work. Caddy escorts the party to Miss Flite's in Krook's Warehouse, where Caddy is practising housekeeping. Mr Woodcourt, the doctor Esther met at Mr Bayham Badger's, is treating Miss Flite's illness, and Krook introduces himself to Mr Jarndyce, and reveals that he is trying to teach himself to read.

Commentary

Dickens continues to examine parent-child relationships, and, while reminding the reader of Mrs Jellyby's irresponsibility, introduces another unsatisfactory parent, Mr Turveydrop, whose indolent reliance on his son's industry is not unlike Skimpole's character. Caddy, by contrast, is learning to develop responsibility by housekeeping for Miss Flite. The names of Miss Flite's birds are symbolical, of course, suggesting the methods, victims and results of Chancery's delays.

Chapter 15

Summary

Skimpole visits Mr Jarndyce in London and tells him that Neckett from

'Coavinses' (a debtor's lock-up house) has died, leaving his three children orphans. Jarndyce, Esther and Ada find them in a room in Bell Yard, with thirteen-year-old Charley working to support five-year-old Tom and baby Emma. Their landlady excuses them their rent and a neighbour, Mr Gridley, sometimes helps them. He is a farmer from Shropshire and tells Jarndyce he has been ruined by a suit in Chancery that has lasted twenty-five years.

Commentary
The appalling poverty of the orphans Charley, Tom and Emma is powerfully evoked in this chapter, and contrasted with the unhelpful charity of such people as Mrs Pardiggle. Charley shows a moving responsibility towards her brother and sister, however, and even Mrs Blinder and poor Mr Gridley offer to help. Though Dickens distrusts institutions, which have, after all, ruined Gridley, his faith in individual goodness, even in the most depressed circumstances, is boundless.

Chapter 16

Summary
Lady Dedlock is restless and visits London while Sir Leicester remains at Chesney Wold. Jo, the crossing-sweeper, lodges in the slum of Tom-all-Alone's, and exists on meagre earnings. One evening a veiled lady asks him to show her Nemo's workplace, home and burial-ground, and gives him a gold coin for helping her. Mrs Rouncewell hears the ghost's steps very clearly at Chesney Wold that evening.

Commentary
The behaviour of the veiled lady creates great suspense in this chapter, and the reader is again invited to become a detective and guess her identity and motives. The way the action moves between Chesney Wold, Tom-all-Alone's, Tulkinghorn's chambers, the places associated with Nemo, and then returns to Chesney Wold not only gives pace to the narrative, but is also the device Dickens uses to remind the reader that all these places and the people in them are connected with each other. Thus Tulkinghorn's Allegory points ironically to the unknown veiled lady outside. Dickens also reveals that Jo's miserable lodgings actually belong to the Court of Chancery, which should protect the poor.

Chapter 17

Summary
Richard is not happy studying medicine and reveals that he would rather study law. Mr Jarndyce suggests that he gives it a trial before making any

decision. Esther is depressed by this and busies herself in work. Mr Jarndyce tells her how he became her guardian when a lady wrote to him for help nine years earlier. Mr Woodcourt comes to take his leave, as he is going to become a ship's surgeon. His mother boasts that he is descended from an illustrious Welsh family and must marry someone of noble birth, but after they have gone Caddy brings Esther some flowers he left her.

Commentary
Richard's growing indecisiveness is contrasted with the way Esther has survived her unhappy childhood and busies herself with good works. Mrs Woodcourt is another parent whose behaviour is scrutinised in the novel, and she painfully reminds Esther of her illegitimacy. Allan's love for Esther is revealed, and, it is suggested, Mr Jarndyce's feelings are not entirely paternal.

Chapter 18

Summary
Richard begins work in Kenge's law-office, and Mr Jarndyce takes Ada, Esther and Skimpole to stay with Boythorn in Lincolnshire. Boythorn greets them warmly, but is still very angry with Sir Leicester Dedlock. At church in the park at Chesney Wold Esther is startled when she sees Lady Dedlock. A few days later, Lady Dedlock speaks to Mr Jarndyce and his party when they are sheltering from a storm in a keeper's lodge, and Ada mistakes her voice for Esther's. When the carriage takes Lady Dedlock and Rosa back to the house, her maid Hortense is left behind to walk back.

Commentary
Esther's first sight of Lady Dedlock and the strange feelings she experiences are the main features of this chapter, and Dickens hints at possible explanations by his references to Esther's childhood use of 'a little glass,' and to the similarities of their voices. Dickens's use of the *déjà vu* technique, is again prominent, for Lady Dedlock has long featured in the novel, but not been seen by Esther. Chesney Wold was also described by the impersonal narrator as early as Chapter 2, though in different terms from Esther's enthusiastic account.

Chapter 19

Summary
During the summer vacation when the law-courts are closed, Mr and Mrs Snagsby invite the clergyman, Chadband, and his wife for tea. The meal is interrupted by a policeman who has arrested Jo for not moving on, and has

come to inquire if Mr Snagsby knows him. Snagsby explains Jo's part in
Nemo's inquest, and Jo describes how a veiled lady gave him a sovereign
for showing her where Nemo lived and is buried. The story intrigues
Mr Guppy, and he also discovers that Mrs Chadband was once in charge of
Esther Summerson. Mr Chadband promises Jo a moral discourse and he is
set free.

Commentary

Dickens shows Guppy learning about the veiled lady, about Nemo, and
about Esther's childhood – like Tulkinghorn, he is one of several amateur
detectives in the novel – and the reader wants to know the explanation of
these intriguing mysteries, too. Dickens also returns to the subject of Jo's
appalling plight, and reveals that lawyers are on holiday, and clergymen
such as Chadband, while over-eating themselves, only offer Jo pompous
platitudes. Significantly, it is Snagsby who offers Jo real food.

Chapter 20

Summary

Mr Guppy is suspicious of Richard Carstone's arrival in Kenge's law-office,
but one day in the summer vacation he and his colleague Bart Smallweed
are visited by his friend Jobling, who is depressed at being out of work.
Guppy and Smallweed take Jobling out for a meal and suggest he does legal
copying for Mr Snagsby and that he obtains cheap lodgings at Mr Krook's,
which will also enable him to spy on Krook. Jobling agrees, and moves
into the lodgings under the assumed name of Weevle.

Commentary

Though Guppy, Smallweed and Jobling are the source of much comedy in
the novel, with Guppy's love-affair particularly satirised by Dickens, they
all have important parts to play in unravelling the novel's mysteries. (Is
Guppy more alert in the third-person narration than in Esther's narrative?)
Jobling's confident hope that 'things will come round' is another example
of irresponsibility, and parallels the worrying information about Richard
in this chapter.

Chapter 21

Summary

Bart Smallweed lives with his twin sister Judy and his aged grandparents in
an unsavoury district near Mount Pleasant. The whole family is devoted to
schemes to make money, and they ill-treat their young maid, Charley.
Trooper George, a military-looking man, comes to pay interest on some

money he had borrowed, and Grandfather Smallweed says he would have made money if he had helped to find a missing person, Captain Hawdon. But George is glad he did not help, fearing that Hawdon would have been imprisoned for debt, and believing that he is already dead. After smoking a pipe with the Smallweeds, George makes his way home to his shooting gallery near Leicester Square.

Commentary

New characters, the Smallweeds and Trooper George, are introduced, who are to have important bearings on the plot, though the connection between Hawdon and earlier events is still obscure at this stage. The Smallweed family are among Dickens's most powerful examples of the grotesque in *Bleak House*, the grandfather's treatment of his aged wife being both comical and frightening. In a novel which frequently discusses the relationship between parents and children, the Smallweeds also stand out because of their rejection of childhood (and fairy tales) and their obsession with money.

Chapter 22

Summary

Mr Tulkinghorn hears the story from Mr Snagsby of Jo's encounter with the veiled lady, and sends him and a detective, Mr Bucket, to fetch Jo to his chambers. They make their way through foul, fever-ridden streets to Tom-all-Alone's, where they have some conversation with Jenny and Liz and their brickmaker-husbands, before they find Jo. At Tulkinghorn's he identifies a veiled lady as the one who questioned him about Nemo until he realises that her hands and voice are different. She is, in fact, Lady Dedlock's former maid Hortense! Jo and Hortense leave, and Bucket urges Snagsby to say nothing of the night's events.

Commentary

At the narrative level detective Bucket begins to try to discover the identity of the veiled lady who was so interested in Nemo – and the reader joins in the detective work, too. At the social level Dickens continues to depict the appalling conditions of the poor, with the apparently fortuitous reintroduction of the brickmakers whom Esther helped earlier. The enigmatic characters of Tulkinghorn and Hortense are exposed to further scrutiny.

Chapter 23

Summary

Esther returns from the holiday at Boythorn's during which she declined

Hortense's offer to become her maid. Richard is less interested in becoming a lawyer and more and more dependent on a successful outcome of the Chancery case. Esther helps Caddy and Prince to tell old Mr Turveydrop that they want to marry and he consents, but Mrs Jellyby is too immersed in her philanthropic correspondence even to be upset by the news! Esther acquires a maid, Charley Neckett, and weeps at Mr Jarndyce's kindness.

Commentary
The contrasting selfishness of two parents is the main focus of this chapter, with Mrs Jellyby's sublime indifference to Caddy's future (or her husband's bankruptcy) and old Mr Turveydrop's vain complacency exposed equally. Richard's moral decline is becoming more pronounced, and he even begins to sound like Miss Flite. Hortense's odd behaviour raises more questions about the mystery of the relationship between Esther and Lady Dedlock.

Chapter 24

Summary
Richard decides to make his career in the army, but he and Mr Jarndyce quarrel over his engagement to Ada. Trooper George gives Richard fencing lessons and seems to recognise Esther, although they have never met. Esther accompanies Richard to Chancery to hear *Jarndyce* and *Jarndyce* discussed, but the case is referred back. Mr Guppy introduces Esther to Mrs Chadband, whom Esther recognises as Mrs Rachel, her godmother's servant. George reveals that he has been hiding Gridley, who is wanted by the police and is very ill. Miss Flite accompanies Esther and George to the shooting gallery, where the physician summoned by George proves to be Inspector Bucket in disguise, but Gridley dies before he can be arrested.

Commentary
Richard, who is increasingly placing his confidence in Chancery, is contrasted with Gridley who has been destroyed by it in this chapter. George's apparent recognition of Esther leads the reader to speculate on the person he may be thinking of, and his reference to the customers at his shooting gallery also contains a clue to future developments. Esther's reunion with Mrs Rachel is another example of the way almost all the characters in the novel cross and recross each other's paths, and Dickens's ambiguous treatment of Bucket is also noticeable.

Chapter 25

Summary
Mr Snagsby cannot help thinking of Detective Bucket, Tulkinghorn and Jo,

and believing that he is a party to a dangerous secret without knowing what it is. Mrs Snagsby becomes suspicious of her husband's behaviour and decides that he is Jo's father. Mr Chadband preaches sanctimoniously to Jo one evening, and, though he reduces Mrs Snagsby to hysterics, makes no impression on Jo. When Jo leaves, Mr Snagsby presents him with another half-crown and his orphaned servant Guster gives him some food.

Commentary

Mr Snagsby plays the part of an amateur detective in speculating on the mysterious behaviour of the real detective Bucket, and this leads his wife to become comically suspicious of his own behaviour. The main source of comedy in this chapter, however, is Dickens's marvellously satirical account of Chadband's bombastic preaching, which ignores Jo's real needs. Significantly, it is Snagsby and the pathetic Guster who offer Jo genuine help.

Chapter 26

Summary

Trooper George and his battered assistant Phil Squod talk about the days when Phil worked for a tinker, and Phil describes how he came by his many injuries. Grandfather Smallweed and Judy visit the shooting gallery to see if George has any of Captain Hawdon's papers. When Smallweed advertised for information about Hawdon (because the captain owed him money) a lawyer saw the advertisement and asked for examples of Hawdon's handwriting. Without revealing whether he has any papers, George accompanies the Smallweeds to the lawyer's office.

Commentary

The intricacy of connecting relationships is emphasised again, when Grandfather Smallweed pursues the matter of handwriting, already referred to as early as Lady Dedlock's shocked recognition of some in Chapter 2. George's reminiscences of his mother and Grandfather Smallweed's hopes of obtaining money from Richard Carstone point to other links in the novel, too. Though Dickens continues to indict irresponsibility and greed, he shows how responsibility and tenderness can survive in the most unlikely places – in the cheerful behaviour of Phil Squod and the brisk conscientiousness of Trooper George. The account of George's careful ablutions parallels the homemaking skills of Esther, and is another way of symbolising order, perhaps.

Chapter 27

Summary
The lawyer Tulkinghorn offers George five guineas for an example of Captain Hawdon's handwriting. George refuses to co-operate but promises to consult an old army friend. He makes his way across London to a musician's shop in the Elephant and Castle district where he has dinner with the Bagnets, but they advise George not to become involved in matters he does not understand. When he tells Tulkinghorn of his decision, the disappointed lawyer blames George for sheltering Gridley, whom he calls a 'murderous, dangerous fellow'. The angry words are heard by a passing clerk.

Commentary
This chapter continues to unfold the mystery of Hawdon's identity and his connection with Lady Dedlock, and further complications are engendered by Tulkinghorn's angry words at the close. The Bagnets represent another force for responsibility and love in the novel, and Mrs Bagnet's housekeeping almost has a symbolic quality. Dickens treats the Bagnets with comic affection, for, though they represent one of the happiest marriages in the novel, Mr Bagnet obviously feels the need to pretend that he is in charge, rather than his wife!

Chapter 28

Summary
While Sir Leicester and Lady Dedlock are entertaining some of their poorer cousins at Chesney Wold, Mrs Rouncewell's son, a prosperous iron-manufacturer, calls. Believing that his son is in love with the maid Rosa, he wishes her to be better educated. Sir Leicester resents the inference that the education of the village school is not good enough for a manufacturer's daughter-in-law and breaks off the discussion. That evening Lady Dedlock treats Rosa with great kindness and is in a thoughtful mood.

Commentary
The main purpose of this chapter is to expose the complacent and class-ridden basis of Victorian society by contrasting Sir Leicester and his poor indolent cousins with the successful industrialist, Rouncewell, whose mother is only a servant. Sir Leicester sees the desire for better education for his wife's maid as threatening social revolution, though it is typical of Dickens's genius that he scrupulously indicates Sir Leicester's good manners during the angry scene. In her kindness to Rosa, Lady Dedlock is perhaps thinking of how she might have had a daughter like her.

Chapter 29

Summary
The young lawyer, Guppy, visits Lady Dedlock at her house in London. He tells her how he noticed a resemblance between Lady Dedlock's portrait and Esther Summerson, and how, through meeting Mrs Chadband, he has learned Esther's real name is Esther Hawdon. He reveals that he has discovered that the dead writer (Nemo) was Hawdon, and that he left some old letters. Lady Dedlock asks Guppy to bring her the letters, and, after he has gone, breaks down and weeps, for she realises that Esther is her own child.

Commentary
Guppy's brilliant detective work has solved the mystery of the connection between Nemo, Lady Dedlock and Esther, and explained a good deal of what has happened earlier in the novel. Suspense is still maintained, however, because the reader wants to know what the consequences of this knowledge will be. What use will Guppy make of his discoveries? What effect will they have on Lady Dedlock? What will happen to Esther? Though Tulkinghorn does not appear in this chapter, there is an ominous reference to him in the third paragraph.

Chapter 30

Summary
Mrs Woodcourt visits Bleak House and reminds Esther of her family's noble lineage, as well as suggesting that her son's attentions should not be taken too seriously. Caddy Jellyby announces that she is to be married in a month's time, and Esther and Ada help her complete the arrangements for the wedding, particularly tidying up the lodgings in Hatton Garden where the Jellybys have lived since Mr Jellyby's bankruptcy. The wedding goes off successfully and Esther hopes the marriage will too.

Commentary
This chapter concentrates on the different attitudes of three sets of parents, Mrs Woodcourt, old Mr Turveydrop and the Jellybys, all of them, except Mr Jellyby, exhibiting a certain amount of selfishness or indifference to their children's future happiness. Some readers find Esther's picture of herself irritating, but her upbringing has given her such a sense of inadequacy that even Mrs Woodcourt's talk makes her uncomfortable. She cannot trust herself to look directly at the implications of what this apparently kind woman is saying because it might expose her real feelings for Allan.

Chapter 31

Summary

Esther's maid, Charley, has met the brickmakers' wives, who have returned to St Albans from London, and are nursing a poor boy. Esther and Charley visit the brickmakers' cottage, where the sick boy, revealed as Jo the crossing-sweeper, confuses Esther with another veiled lady. They take him back to Bleak House to nurse him but he disappears in the night. Charley catches the boy's fever but Esther nurses her back to health. Then Esther herself falls ill and goes blind.

Commentary

The appalling condition of Jo and the other unfortunates is reiterated, and the loving care of Esther and Charley sharply contrasted with the frivolous irresponsibility of Skimpole. Jo's first appearance in Esther's narrative is another example of the *déjà vu* effect. Another feature of this chapter is what happens to Esther. She feels a great change come over her, and it may be that the illness (usually regarded as smallpox) which changes her appearance is a physical sign of her moral and psychological change, as she begins to learn more about the circumstances of her illegitimate birth.

Chapter 32

Summary

Late one night, Snagsby encounters Weevle (alias Jobling) outside Krook's warehouse where they discuss the unpleasant atmosphere. Guppy joins Weevle, who confesses that he has had a fit of the horrors. Weevle has engaged to meet Krook at midnight to help him examine letters sent to Hawdon, which Krook himself is unable to read. Guppy complains about soot in Weevle's room and about a sickening yellow oil running down Weevle's walls. When Weevle goes to collect Krook's papers, Krook is not there. There is a smouldering, suffocating vapour in the room and a burnt patch on the floor, and Krook has died from a spontaneous combustion!

Commentary

Though readers have criticised the literal credibility of this chapter, its power and intensity give it an unforgettable quality. Guppy and Weevle are conspiring to get hold of papers dishonestly, which will be to their advantage, papers which Krook himself acquired dishonestly and hopes to turn to his own profit. None of them is concerned with the effect of his behaviour upon other people. Guppy and Weevle are both associated with the legal profession, and Krook is known as the Lord Chancellor, and so this chapter mirrors in a way that irresponsible manoeuvring associated, in

Dickens's view, not just with the Court of Chancery but many other aspects of British society. The vividly described scene of horror then works perfectly as a symbol of what all the anti-social forces at work in the novel may cause – a revolutionary explosion.

Chapter 33

Summary
There is great agitation in the region of Chancery Lane over Krook's death, and Mrs Snagsby is very suspicious of her husband's interest. Guppy and Weevle decide to say nothing about Hawdon's letters in their evidence at the inquest, but Weevle indignantly rejects Guppy's suggestion that he should go on living at the warehouse in order to search Krook's possessions. The Smallweeds arrive for the inquest and, revealing that Krook was Mrs Smallweed's brother, are granted possession of his property. A disappointed Guppy tells Lady Dedlock that the letters he was going to bring her have been destroyed, and meets Tulkinghorn, who is also Smallweed's lawyer, as he leaves.

Commentary
Just when the reader believes that Krook's death has ended one line of development in the novel, Dickens opens up the possibility of a new one by revealing more unexpected relationships in the connections between Krook and the Smallweeds, and between the Smallweeds and Tulkinghorn. Characteristically, the Smallweeds were not 'on terms' with Krook. Lady Dedlock's relief may be only temporary, too, as Tulkinghorn's brooding presence suggests.

Chapter 34

Summary
Trooper George receives a letter from Smallweed telling him that his loan must be repaid the next day, and George is worried because he cannot repay it and suspects that, if it is not extended, his guarantor Bagnet will have to pay it. He and Bagnet ask Smallweed for help in their difficulty, but, after receiving them pleasantly, he threatens to smash them, and refers them to his lawyer, Tulkinghorn. Mrs Rouncewell is engaged with the lawyer when they arrive, but Tulkinghorn agrees to help George in exchange for Hawdon's letter, which George had previously refused to sell him. Though the Bagnets celebrate the good news that evening, George is very depressed.

Commentary
Smallweed and Tulkinghorn, in pursuit of a letter from Hawdon, continue to tangle honest Trooper George and the Bagnets in their wiles, and Mrs Bagnet's cheerful character shines out amid all the intrigues. The examination of parent-child relationships here focuses on the Bagnet family, but Trooper George's avoidance of Mrs Rouncewell, and his advice to young Woolwich, hint at less happy examples. The coincidence of his mother being at the lawyer's office when Trooper George arrives is given some credibility by the fact that Tulkinghorn is Lady Dedlock's lawyer, but the meeting is another example of the way Dickens reveals the interdependence of so many apparently unconnected events.

Chapter 25

Summary
Esther recovers from her illness, but the absence of a mirror from her room makes her realise that her face is disfigured. She asks her guardian's permission to go into the country for a week before showing herself again, and he tells her that Richard is becoming even more dependent on the outcome of the Chancery case. Miss Flite visits Esther and reveals that a veiled lady took the handkerchief Esther had left at the brickmakers' cottage. Miss Flite talks of her family's tragic involvement with the Court of Chancery, and tells Esther that news has arrived of Allan Woodcourt's heroism during a shipwreck in the East Indian ocean. Esther confesses to the reader that she once thought he loved her but is glad he never declared his feelings, as she will not have to tell him of her facial disfigurement.

Commentary
The tragic dependence on the Court of Chancery which destroyed Miss Flite's family, and which increasingly threatens Richard, is paralleled in this chapter by news of the devastating effects of the disease that reaches from Tom-all-Alone's to Esther. The veiled lady is referred to again, as Lady Dedlock tries to discover more about her daughter. The way Esther constantly strives to overcome difficulties, suggested by the symbolism of her dream of 'colossal staircases', is another indication that her character is more complicated than it appears superficially.

Chapter 36

Summary
Esther and Charley holiday at Boythorn's house in Lincolnshire, and Esther sees how much the illness has disfigured her face. One day in the park-woods at Chesney Wold Lady Dedlock approaches, and confesses she is her

mother. She had believed Esther died at birth and only recently learned of her survival. Terrified that her disgrace will be revealed to her husband, she urges Esther to keep her secret, and they embrace for the last time. Ada and Jarndyce arrive, and Ada's love for Esther, despite her scarred face, reassures her.

Commentary
Though the mystery of Lady Dedlock's connection with Esther is solved, Dickens raises other questions such as whether Tulkinghorn will also discover the secret and reveal it to Sir Leicester. Esther's realisation of her true identity is matched by the discovery of her new appearance, but, though she is threatened by feelings of guilt again, as the cause of her mother's disgrace, she recovers a sense of innocence and responds bravely to her difficult situation.

Chapter 37

Summary
Richard arrives unexpectedly. He has become deeply involved in the Chancery case and tells Esther he has decided to break with Mr Jarndyce because he is an interested party. Esther is alarmed by this and by Richard's growing friendship with Skimpole, but she gives the news to Ada, who writes to Richard advising him to give up the Chancery case and defending Mr Jarndyce's character. Though Richard reasserts his love for Ada, Esther suspects that the case is even affecting this. A new lawyer, Mr Vholes, arrives and tells Richard that his cause is to be discussed in Chancery the next day, and he and Richard leave for London.

Commentary
The main emphasis in this chapter is on Richard's continued decline, his preoccupation with Chancery now leading to debt and the break with Mr Jarndyce, and even threatening his love for Ada. Mr Vholes is a deathly, predatory figure of the law, but his concern for his daughters and aged father show that he does not represent pure evil. Is he rather a merciless operator of an inhuman system? Esther's confrontation with Skimpole reveals his selfishness, though he perceptively calls her 'the very touchstone of responsibility'.

Chapter 38

Summary
When Esther returns to Bleak House, she visits London, where she finds Caddy happily married and learning to give dancing-lessons as Prince's

health is not good. Together Esther and Caddy call on Mr Guppy, and Esther begs him not to make any further inquiries about her personal history. Guppy, startled by Esther's changed appearance, and fearing that she wishes to take up his proposal of marriage, is clumsily anxious to hear her formally decline his offer again in front of Caddy.

Commentary
The main contrast in this chapter is between the wholesome, loving nature of Caddy, who is cheerfully working hard to support her husband and family, and that of Guppy, who is only too anxious to withdraw his proposal to Esther, though he is ashamed of his feelings when he discovers the real purpose of Esther's visit.

Chapter 39

Summary
Mr Vholes, in his office in Symond's Inn, promises Richard he will work tirelessly on his behalf, and obtains twenty pounds on account. Guppy and Weevle watch Richard cross Lincoln's Inn Square, and then visit Krook's warehouse, where the Smallweeds have taken possession, to collect Weevle's belongings. Tulkinghorn congratulates Guppy on knowing the nobility and admires his portrait of Lady Dedlock.

Commentary
This chapter is full of spies as Guppy and Weevle, Tulkinghorn and the Smallweeds all keep an eye on each other's activities, and in this way Dickens continues to create an atmosphere of suspense. The personality of Vholes is very striking. He is presented as 'a very respectable man' and a loving son and father, but his business is English Law, whose principle is 'to make business for itself'. He is also compared to such predators as a fox and a cat. Is Dickens suggesting that he, too, is the victim of a merciless system, or that he is a consummate villain? Richard's decline continues, and when Weevle compares him with Krook, saying Richard is a case of 'smouldering combustion', he reminds the reader of other tragic figures.

Chapter 40

Summary
When Lord Coodle resigns, Sir Thomas Doodle succeeds him as Prime Minister after a delay of several weeks. He calls a General Election and the Dedlocks return to Chesney Wold. Tulkinghorn tells Sir Leicester that he has been beaten, and that Rouncewell the ironmaster was very active against him in the election. He also tells the story of how a townsman of

Rouncewell's took his daughter away from working for a wealthy lady, when it was discovered that the lady had had an illegitimate baby by an army captain. Lady Dedlock seems unmoved by the story.

Commentary
In the opening of this chapter Dickens satirises the political system of mid-Victorian England for its arrogant assumptions about who was fit to become Prime Minister, and the way candidates bribed the electors with money and beer. Injustice is not confined to Parliament or Chancery, however, and the second part of the chapter emphasises Tulkinghorn's personal cruelty, as he tells a story deliberately to torment Lady Dedlock.

Chapter 41

Summary
Lady Dedlock confronts Tulkinghorn and asks him why he has told her story, and he explains that it was necessary she should know he had discovered her secret. Lady Dedlock plans to fly in disgrace but Tulkinghorn forbids her, claiming that his concern is Sir Leicester's welfare and that news of her disgrace and flight would cause him great pain. Lady Dedlock agrees to do nothing until Tulkinghorn has decided what action he will take.

Commentary
At last Tulkinghorn breaks down Lady Dedlock's composure, for his knowledge of her secret gives him great power over her. His motives are not revealed, however, and it looks as if he simply enjoys the power to manipulate people for its own sake. The reader cannot help speculating on what he will do with his power, however, or how Lady Dedlock will respond.

Chapter 42

Summary
Tulkinghorn returns to London and Snagsby visits his chambers to complain that Hortense, Lady Dedlock's ex-maid, has been calling at his shop in search of Tulkinghorn, and making his wife very jealous. Later, Hortense calls on the lawyer himself and complains that the money he paid her for helping him identify the veiled lady as Lady Dedlock was not enough. She demands that Tulkinghorn should find her a new post or employ her to help disgrace Lady Dedlock, but Tulkinghorn is unmoved, and threatens Hortense with prison if she pesters him or Snagsby again.

Commentary
Tulkinghorn's plotting against Lady Dedlock has created other

complications, and he now has a dissatisfied accomplice to deal with. In view of the way suspicion for the murder later falls on Lady Dedlock, the reader needs to see Snagsby's apparently comic reference to 'a foreign dagger' as another clue towards solving the mystery. In a chapter dealing with such intrigues, it is appropriate that the figure of Allegory is almost invisible, but Dickens tells us that he is still at his old work, pointing lessons, and perhaps anticipating Tulkinghorn's death.

Chapter 43

Summary

Mr Jarndyce, Esther and Ada, concerned about Richard, visit Skimpole in London, and urge him not to take any more money from Richard. Esther is dismayed by Skimpole's dingy house and irresponsible way of living, but he accompanies them back to Bleak House, leaving his wife and daughters to deal with an angry debtor. Sir Leicester calls on Jarndyce to assure him that he and his friends are welcome to visit Chesney Wold, despite the quarrel with Boythorn. Esther is startled by this meeting with her mother's husband and decides to tell her guardian what she knows. He reveals that Boythorn nearly married Lady Dedlock's sister, and Esther confesses that Lady Dedlock is her mother.

Commentary

Skimpole's irresponsibility and its damaging effect upon Richard is the main subject of the first half of this chapter, and Skimpole's treatment of his children compares with other parent-child relationships in the novel. Sir Leicester's visit threatens not only to embarrass Esther, but in revealing the connection between Boythorn, Miss Barbary and Esther opens up another web of relationships in the novel.

Chapter 44

Summary

Esther completes her confession and her guardian tells her that he does not think she need fear exposure from Mr Guppy or Hortense. Jarndyce is grateful to Esther for the changes she has brought to his life, and asks if he may write her an important letter. In it he proposes marriage, not only to show his love, but also in order to prove that the prediction made about her in her childhood was false. Esther feels she must accept her guardian's proposal and devote the rest of her life to his happiness. But she cries very much as she feels she is losing something, and that night she burns the withered flowers Allan Woodcourt once gave her. After delaying for two weeks, she tells Mr Jarndyce that she will marry him.

Commentary
Though the mystery of Esther's birth has now been solved, the reader's interest is maintained by uncertainties about whether Lady Dedlock's secret will be exposed. Jarndyce's proposal raises problems for Esther, too. She loves and respects her guardian, and prudence suggests the marriage would be a good one, but Esther is a young woman with powerful emotions, which she recognises that marriage to Jarndyce would not fulfil.

Chapter 45

Summary
Vholes announces that Richard is falling further into debt and thinking of leaving the army, so Esther travels to Deal, where Richard is stationed, to see if she can help. She delivers a letter from Ada offering her small inheritance if Richard will stay in the army but he declines her generous offer, and blames Jarndyce for separating them. He is returning to London to pursue his Chancery case. Esther recognises Allan Woodcourt among a group of sailors just landing and sends him a note, asking him to meet her. He seems very sorry at her changed appearance, but speaks kindly, and promises to befriend Richard in London.

Commentary
Richard's decline is emphasised and his character contrasted with that of the good surgeon, Allan Woodcourt. Some readers find Esther's chance encounter with him an unconvincing coincidence, but it can also be seen as Dickens's way of showing how characters cannot escape their pasts. Esther's willingness to confront Allan, despite her disfigured face, is a sign of her growing maturity, but her lack of self-confidence might still be present in the way she interprets his reaction.

Chapter 46

Summary
Walking through Tom-all-Alone's late one night Allan Woodcourt encounters a brickmaker's wife (whom the reader identifies as Jenny) on a doorstep, and treats her bruised forehead. She runs after the ragged boy Jo and when Allan catches him, he learns that Jo was nursed by Esther, to whom he gave the smallpox, but that he ran away from Bleak House on the order of a mysterious man.

Commentary
Dickens emphasises the interdependence of all members of society in this chapter, first by describing the way the wind spreads diseases from

Tom-all-Alone's all over the country, and then by showing how the apparently coincidental meeting of Woodcourt, Jenny and Jo reveals all kinds of connections not only between them, but with Esther, Snagsby and Nemo, and through them with the Dedlocks and Tulkinghorn, and so many characters in the whole novel. Thus the chapter mirrors the theme of *Bleak House* as a whole. The irresponsible neglect of one individual or one aspect of society can damage everyone, even if they are not obviously connected with each other. The *déjà vu* effect is also noticeable in this chapter as Allan meets a character, Jenny, whom the reader has already encountered several times earlier.

Chapter 47

Summary
Allan Woodcourt searches for lodgings for Jo, who is very ill, and Miss Flite eventually leads him to Trooper George's shooting gallery. George agrees to shelter Jo, and suggests that it was Detective Bucket who made Jo leave Bleak House. He tells Allan of Jo's history, and about the meeting with Tulkinghorn, whom he angrily denounces. Woodcourt communicates his discoveries to Mr Jarndyce, but though everyone tries to help Jo, he dies while reciting the Lord's Prayer.

Commentary
Dickens's account of Jo's death is one of his most powerful pieces of writing, but the emotions behind it are not simply pity for the unfortunate boy but anger at a society whose neglect and irresponsibility allow it to happen. The last sentence of the chapter makes it clear that Jo's death was no isolated phenomenon. The ineffective philanthropists and even Detective Bucket are criticised, but Dickens holds Parliament, Chancery and almost all other institutions ultimately responsible. It is the work of kind individuals - Woodcourt, George, Snagsby, even George's servant Phil Squod - which is praised, though George's denunciation of Tulkinghorn is to have painful consequences.

Chapter 48

Summary
Lady Dedlock asks her maid Rosa to leave her service, informing Ironmaster Rouncewell that Rosa is still in love with his grandson. After Rouncewell and Rosa have left, Tulkinghorn accuses Lady Dedlock of breaking their agreement, saying she sent Rosa away to spare her from exposure to Lady Dedlock's disgrace. He declares that he now feels free to tell Sir Leicester of his wife's past, but refuses to say when he will do so. After he has gone,

home, Lady Dedlock also goes out for an evening walk. A gunshot is heard in the night and next morning Tulkinghorn is found murdered in his chambers.

Commentary
Whereas Jo's death was described in detail, Tulkinghorn's murder is presented more obscurely so that the identity of his murderer, which now becomes one of the great mysteries in the second part of the novel, is concealed. Lady Dedlock has motive and opportunity, but detectives need to consider all the evidence before coming to a conclusion. The Roman Allegory now points to Tulkinghorn's body like an important figure of Fate.

Chapter 49

Summary
On Mrs Bagnet's birthday, the whole family celebrates, and Trooper George, though depressed by the death of Jo the day before, brings her a present of a brooch. Detective Bucket, declaring himself a friend of George's, also joins in the celebrations, but when George goes home, Bucket arrests him for the murder of Tulkinghorn.

Commentary
Bucket's arrest of Trooper George for Tulkinghorn's murder reveals another suspect, for angry words had been overheard between Tulkinghorn and George. Bucket's behaviour raises some questions, however. On the one hand, he is shrewd and professional, but the way he wins the affection of the Bagnets, and then arrests George for reward money suggests that he, too, might be accused of being very calculating. The happy Bagnet family contrasts with many other families in the novel, such as, for example, the Smallweeds.

Chapter 50

Summary
When Esther returns to Bleak House from Deal, she learns that Caddy Jellyby is ill, so she, Ada and Mr Jarndyce move to London in order to nurse her. Mr Jarndyce suggests calling in Allan Woodcourt's assistance and Caddy gradually recovers. Esther becomes aware that a change is coming over Ada, who seems troubled but is unable to talk about her problem. Esther notices that Ada sleeps with one hand under her pillow, however.

Commentary
The selfish behaviour of Caddy Jellyby's relations contrasts sharply with

the cheerful account given of the Bagnets in the previous chapter. The shadow that falls across Ada suggests that she, too, is now becoming involved in difficulties associated with Chancery in some way. Jarndyce's discussion of Woodcourt points to future developments.

Chapter 51

Summary
Allan Woodcourt visits Richard in Symond's Inn to find him deteriorating, and Mr Vholes intimates that he needs more money. When Esther and Ada call on Richard, Esther notices his sunken appearance, too. Ada declares that she is not returning to Bleak House and reveals that she and Richard were married two months earlier, as Esther had suspected. Esther breaks the news to Mr Jarndyce and he expresses pity for the couple. Esther feels that she has not been as devoted to her guardian as she might have been.

Commentary
Though this chapter emphasises Richard's mental and physical deterioration, it also reveals Ada's trusting love of him. The relationship between Jarndyce and Esther, on the other hand, remains like that between father and daughter. Indeed Esther refers to her guardian's 'old bright fatherly look'. The opening scene of this chapter actually describes an interview Esther never witnessed, and the fact that it must have been related to her afterwards by Woodcourt suggests a developing relationship there.

Chapter 52

Summary
When news comes of Tulkinghorn's murder, Esther remembers how her mother, Lady Dedlock, never trusted him. Allan Woodcourt, Jarndyce and Esther visit Trooper George in prison and assert their belief in his innocence. He refuses to employ a lawyer to defend himself, however, declaring he would rather be hanged than use one. The Bagnets fail to change his mind, too, but Mrs Bagnet resolves to bring his mother down from Lincolnshire to persuade him.

Commentary
Allan Woodcourt summarises the evidence against Trooper George, emphasising his animosity towards Tulkinghorn and his appearance at the scene of the crime, but Esther remembers her mother's fear of the lawyer and is startled to hear that a woman like her was present on the fatal night. Thus Dickens creates suspense by suggesting two possible murderers. Trooper George's refusal to employ a lawyer is another aspect of Dickens's

treatment of the law in the novel. Characteristically, it is the humble but stout-hearted Mrs Bagnet who offers practical help.

Chapter 53

Summary
Mr Bucket attends Tulkinghorn's funeral and is employed by Sir Leicester to find the murderer. He receives half a dozen anonymous letters accusing Lady Dedlock and tells Sir Leicester he believes that the case will be solved in a few hours. By questioning one of the servants he establishes that Lady Dedlock went out walking on the night of the murder, wearing a loose, black mantle.

Commentary
Detective Bucket's apparently casual investigation seems to suggest that Lady Dedlock killed Tulkinghorn, but there are several ironies in this chapter, as when Sir Leicester declares that he would not spare the culprit, even if he were his brother! Artfully, Dickens gives Mrs Bucket and her lodger only the briefest mention.

Chapter 54

Summary
Next morning, Detective Bucket tells Sir Leicester that his wife is involved in the case. Tulkinghorn had discovered that she had once had a lover and there was bad blood between Lady Dedlock and the lawyer as a result of his discovery. Bucket also reveals that Lady Dedlock went out to visit Tulkinghorn on the night of his murder. At this point, Grandfather Smallweed, Mr and Mrs Chadband and Mrs Snagsby suddenly arrive. Smallweed has discovered Lady Dedlock's letter to her lover and wants five hundred pounds to keep it secret. Bucket sends them away, promising to call on them shortly, and advises Sir Leicester to buy their silence. He then introduces Hortense, Lady Dedlock's former maid, and exposes her as Tulkinghorn's killer. She had bitterly resented being discharged by Lady Dedlock and thought she had a claim on Tulkinghorn. When he refused further help, she shot him, but was seen by Mrs Bucket, when lodging at their house, writing the letters accusing Lady Dedlock of the crime. Sir Leicester is shattered by the news, for he has always loved his wife deeply.

Commentary
The revelation of the murderer's real identity is very startling on a first reading of the novel, for Dickens has cleverly suggested several other suspects. The arrival of Smallweed's party reminds the reader, however, that many other characters in the novel have also played the part of

amateur detective besides the painstaking Bucket. Now that the novel's second great mystery is solved, new questions arise. What effect will the disclosure of Lady Dedlock's secret have?

Chapter 55

Summary

Meanwhile, Mrs Bagnet has visited Mrs Rouncewell, Trooper George's mother, at Chesney Wold, and brought her back to London, where she is reunited with her long-lost son. She persuades him to obtain legal aid and he agrees, but asks her not to let his brother know of his situation. Mrs Rouncewell then calls on Lady Dedlock at her London home and asks her for help, producing an anonymous letter which accuses Lady Dedlock of the murder. Guppy warns Lady Dedlock that the Smallweeds have her lover's letters, and may have brought them to the house. Realising that her secret is known to all, Lady Dedlock writes her husband a farewell note, asking him to forget her, and then veils herself and leaves the house.

Commentary

The moving reconciliation of Mrs Rouncewell with her son is another illustration of parent-child relationships in the novel, a theme which is also touched on ironically when Mrs Rouncewell wonders if Lady Dedlock can imagine her maternal feelings. The theme of the law also re-emerges when Mrs Bagnet compares truth and justice with law and lawyers. Lady Dedlock's flight now becomes the major cause of suspense in the novel's last chapters.

Chapter 56

Summary

Sir Leicester suffers a stroke and can only communicate with Mrs Rouncewell by writing. She shows him Lady Dedlock's letter and he summons Bucket to search for her and offer his full forgiveness. The detective finds Esther's handkerchief in Lady Dedlock's boudoir and calls on Mr Jarndyce late at night to beg for Esther's help in his search.

Commentary

With the discovery of Lady Dedlock's flight, the narrative gains pace as Dickens suggests the desperate speed of Bucket's search, and in the last paragraph the reference to the brick-kilns hints at the final twist in the unfolding of Lady Dedlock's tragedy. Bucket's meeting with Esther for the first time since Chapter 24 also gives these concluding chapters a peculiar intensity, for the concerns of the third-person narrator coincide with those of the first-person narrator, and Dickens begins to pull all the threads of his wide-ranging plot closer together. Sir Leicester, who has behaved like an arrogant reactionary for most of the novel, now reveals a genuine love of, and forgiveness for, his wife, despite the disgrace she has brought on his family name.

Chapter 57

Summary
Detective Bucket and Esther search London for Lady Dedlock without success and then take a carriage north towards St Albans, with Bucket making inquiries all the way about a woman who left London on foot earlier. (On the way the detective reveals that he was responsible for Jo's abrupt departure from Bleak House as he worried about Jo's talking too much.) Since there have been no new visitors at Bleak House, Esther and Bucket next interrogate the brickmakers, and Liz tells them a lady called the previous day looking pale and exhausted. Jenny has now gone to London but the lady went north. Bucket and Esther pursue her through snow and mist, thinking Lady Dedlock may be making for Boythorn's house in Lincolnshire. But Bucket gradually loses track of the missing woman. He suddenly declares, 'I've got it!' and orders a return to London.

Commentary
The pace of the search for Lady Dedlock is largely suggested by the description of Bucket's tremendous energy, as he drives across London and the countryside, interrogates witnesses, and yet is constantly attentive to Esther. Though Bucket is a sympathetic figure, and Skimpole is exposed for betraying Jo, the detective is not presented uncritically, however, as Esther's cool questioning reveals. By not explaining why Bucket orders the return to London, Dickens asks the reader to think like the detective again.

Chapter 58

Summary
Meanwhile in London, rumours spread about Lady Dedlock's behaviour. Sir Leicester, now ill in bed and grieving for his wife's absence, asks to see George Rouncewell, whom he had known as a boy. Sir Leicester confesses that there has been a slight misunderstanding with his wife but declares that his love for her remains unaltered. Trooper George brings some comfort to the sick baronet as the day passes, but there is no word of Lady Dedlock.

Commentary
After the sharp attack on society gossip at the beginning of this chapter,

Dickens concentrates on the return of Trooper George to his mother, and
the longing of Sir Leicester for his wife's return. Sir Leicester's declaration of
love is particularly moving, after his haughty behaviour earlier in the novel.

Chapter 59

Summary
Bucket and Esther return to London in the early morning and make their
way to Chancery Lane. Here they meet Allan Woodcourt just returning
from visiting Richard, who is not well. He accompanies them to Mr Snagsby's
where Bucket asks Woodcourt's assistance in obtaining a letter from
Guster, who is having a fit. The detective reproves Mrs Snagsby for her
jealous suspicions and Allan produces the letter. In it Lady Dedlock
describes her terrible wanderings, declares she is near death, and begs Esther's
forgiveness. Bucket, Woodcourt and Esther now hasten, on Guster's in-
structions, to Nemo's burial-ground. Esther, still not fully understanding
what has happened, thinks the woman lying on the step is Jenny, but, as
Bucket explains, the two women changed clothes, and Esther discovers her
dead mother.

Commentary
Dickens resolves another of the novel's mysteries with the death of Lady
Dedlock, and Bucket explains why the search for her was so difficult.
Psychologically, the chapter also marks another stage in Esther's moral
development, too, for finding her dead mother perhaps helps her to confront her painful history. Does the dead child she mentions symbolise her
own death as the child of sin? The reference to Richard reminds us of the
unresolved problem of the Chancery case.

Chapter 60

Summary
After the ordeal, Esther is ill for a short period, but when she recovers
Mr Jarndyce invites Mrs Woodcourt to stay with them in London so that
her son can see her more often. Alan brings news of Richard's deterioration,
and Mr Jarndyce tells Esther that Allan is seeking employment as a medical
attendant for the poor in Yorkshire. Esther visits Ada regularly in her
miserable lodgings, and sees how she and Richard are gradually growing
poorer. Miss Flite tells her that Richard attends Chancery so often that she
has added two birds to her collection, calling them the wards in Jarndyce.
Esther sees how thin and languid Richard is, and Mr Vholes tells her that
his affairs are in a very bad way. Ada reaffirms her love of Richard, however, but fears that he may not live to see the child she is expecting.

Commentary

After Lady Dedlock's tragedy, more emphasis is placed on the account of Richard's ruin, which is aided by the sinister figure of Vholes, though he never does anything actually illegal. The reference to Miss Flite's birds suggests disaster cannot be far off, but in the discussion about Allan Woodcourt and his mother Dickens hints at signs of hope elsewhere.

Chapter 61

Summary

Esther feels that Skimpole's visits to Richard are making Richard poorer and Ada unhappy, so she calls on Skimpole and he agrees to stop his visits because he is not enjoying them so much, finding Richard mercenary! Esther also expresses surprise at the way Skimpole betrayed Jo for money, but Skimpole says that he is unbribable – he helped Bucket because he wanted to! Esther reveals that she never saw Skimpole again after this interview. He died five years later, leaving a book in which he described Mr Jarndyce as 'the Incarnation of Selfishness'. Allan Woodcourt continues to help the declining Richard, and when he walks Esther home one night he declares his love for her. Though thrilled by his words, Esther explains her relationship with her guardian.

Commentary

Skimpole's frivolous irresponsibility is contrasted with Allan Woodcourt's loving concern for Richard as his decline continues. Esther's tears at the end of the chapter suggest that she wishes for a fuller relationship than that offered by her guardian, but her engagement seems an insuperable obstacle.

Chapter 62

Summary

The next morning, Esther and her guardian agree to marry in a month's time. Detective Bucket arrives with Grandfather Smallweed and produces a paper found among Krook's property which seems to be a Will. Repudiating any interest in the case, Mr Jarndyce promises to see Mr Smallweed suitably rewarded, and takes the paper to his lawyer, Kenge. He declares that it is a Will of later date than any other in the Jarndyce case, one which advances the interest of Richard and Ada but reduces that of John Jarndyce. Vholes agrees with this interpretation and both lawyers look forward to the case being discussed in court again in a month's time.

Commentary

In a novel where letters, documents and notes are constantly being referred
to, the discovery of a new Will promises to bring an end to the outstanding
affair of *Jarndyce* and *Jarndyce*, and the reader is thus being prepared for
yet another twist in the story. Esther's meeting with Grandfather Smallweed,
who has played a large part in the third-person narrative, is another example
of Dickens's use of the *déjà vu* technique.

Chapter 63

Summary

Trooper George gives up his shooting gallery and becomes Sir Leicester
Dedlock's attendant at Chesney Wold. He rides north into the iron country
and seeks an interview with his brother, the prosperous industrialist, who
greets him warmly and takes him home to celebrate his son's engagement
to Rosa. George asks advice on how he is to persuade his mother to leave
him out of her Will, but his brother dissuades him from pursuing the idea.
George declines his brother's offer of a job, feeling he will be more useful
helping Sir Leicester. The elder brother reads through and agrees to post a
letter from George to Esther explaining how he came to have a letter from
Captain Hawdon, and why he came to believe Hawdon was dead. Promising
to return for Watt's wedding, George rides back to Chesney Wold.

Commentary

Dickens is now resolving various minor elements in the plot, and shows
Trooper George finding a happier way of life, and one which compares not
unfavourably with that of his older brother, whose successful industry
actually blights the landscape. George's letter to Esther and the references
to Rosa tidy up other loose ends, Rosa's engagement being another of those
superb strokes by which Dickens reminds the reader of the complicated
web of relationships in the novel.

Chapter 64

Summary

Mr Jarndyce gives Esther two hundred pounds for her wedding preparations,
and then goes north on Mr Woodcourt's business. Unexpectedly, he asks
Esther to join him and shows her over the cottage, also to be called *Bleak
House*, he has bought for Allan. He then declares that in proposing to marry
her, he had his own interests too much in view, and knows that she will be
happier with Allan. Esther and Allan are united and plan to marry before
the month is out. Mr Guppy, his mother and Weevle call on Esther in
London, however. Guppy is now a qualified lawyer and renews his proposal

to Esther. When Esther rejects him again, his mother becomes noisily abusive.

Commentary

Jarndyce's selfless recognition of the fact that his marriage to Esther would not make her truly happy helps the reader to perceive how much Esther has changed in the novel, though she now reveals that the events described actually happened seven years earlier. Compared with Allan's behaviour, Guppy's proposal is ludicrously worded. He seems more interested in his new home, 'use of fixtures included', than in Esther's feelings.

Chapter 65

Summary

When the Law Term begins, Allan and Esther go down to court to hear the case of *Jarndyce* and *Jarndyce*, but Caddy Jellyby meets them on the way, and, now a successful teacher, insists on stopping to tell Allan how much she owes Esther. Consequently, Allan and Esther arrive late in court and find everyone laughing. The case has ended, and Kenge tells them that the whole estate was found to have been absorbed in its legal costs! Richard is shattered by the news. When Esther and Mr Jarndyce visit him, he praises Allan's goodness, and is reconciled with his guardian. Though weak, he hopes to become stronger and to make a fresh start. He especially looks forward to visiting the new Bleak House Mr Jarndyce has prepared for Allan and Esther. But he is too ill and he dies, begging Ada's forgiveness for the wrongs he has done her. Leter, Miss Flite arrives to say that she has set all her birds free.

Commentary

The collapse of the legal case, which has been one of the dominating concerns of the novel, is the most powerful expression of the irresponsible working of Chancery in the book, for it has created anxiety and despair everywhere, and been the immediate cause of Richard's death. Miss Flite's liberation of her birds reminds the reader of their symbolic names. Caddy's success, on the other hand, functions as a moral contrast to the irresponsibility of Richard and Chancery.

Chapter 66

Summary

Chesney Wold is silent now. Lady Dedlock is buried in the family mausoleum which Sir Leicester visits, accompanied by his servant Trooper George.

Boythorn still quarrels with Sir Leicester over the right of way, but people say that he does it to humour the baronet. Trooper George regularly takes his mother to church and occasionally visits his friends, the Bagnets. The greater part of Chesney Wold is shut up and there is little social life there except for cousin Volumnia's evening-readings to Sir Leicester. The passion and pride of the place have died away.

Commentary
The movement towards inertia, present at Chesney Wold from the novel's beginning, is almost complete, and perhaps symbolises Dickens's view of the Victorian upper classes. The reference to Boythorn, which is amusing in its own right, also reminds the reader of how widely the major themes of the novel have spread, while the mention of Mrs Rouncewell, George and the Bagnets is part of Dickens's tidying-up of various minor threads in the novel.

Chapter 67

Summary
Esther concludes her narrative and reveals that she has been mistress of Bleak House for seven years now. After Richard's death, Ada was ill for several weeks, but had a baby boy, also named Richard, and is now more beautiful than ever. Mr Jarndyce has become guardian of her and her son, and visits Esther regularly. Charley Neckitt is married to a miller, and her sister Emma is now Esther's maid. Caddy Jellyby continues to prosper, though Mrs Jellyby has given up African affairs and is busier than ever in correspondence concerned with the rights of women to sit in Parliament. Old Mr Turveydrop still exhibits his deportment about town and Peepy is doing well in the Custom-House. Esther and Allan are not rich, but earn people's gratitude for the help they give, and Allan insists that Esther is prettier than ever.

Commentary
The novel ends on a note of qualified optimism. Though society's irresponsibility and selfishness destroy or bring grief to many, it is possible for some individuals to achieve happiness, even in the most unpromising circumstances, as Esther, Caddy and Charley have done. A heavy price has to be paid, however, and Esther still shows signs of her old insecurity.

3 THEMES AND ISSUES

3.1 RESPONSIBILITY AND IRRESPONSIBILITY

The action of *Bleak House* is dominated by images of decay and waste, muddle and neglect. A sense of weariness and lethargy pervades the whole book, from the description of the legal delays over *Jarndyce* and *Jarndyce* in the first chapter to the account of a darkening Chesney Wold at the close.

This impression of weariness and defeat is intensified by the presence of so much illness and death in the novel. Nemo, Krook, Tulkinghorn, Gridley, Jo, Lady Dedlock and Richard Carstone all die in extremely dramatic circumstances, and the reader also hears more briefly of the deaths of Esther's godmother – Miss Barbary – and Tom Jarndyce, Mr Neckett and of Jenny's baby. Esther, Charley, Jo and Ada suffer prolonged illnesses in the novel, too – Jo fatally. The name Jarndyce itself sounds like the debilitating illness jaundice.

This decay and death is not confined to one part of England; it permeates all areas. In the first chapter of the novel neglect and fog are described in the High Court of Chancery; in the second chapter, lethargy and stagnant waters dominate Chesney Wold in Lincolnshire; in Chapter 3, Esther's stern upbringing is equally melancholy; in the fourth chapter, the account of Mrs Jellyby's household emphasises the dirtiness of the house and the mother's neglect; and in the fifth chapter, Krook's rag and bottle warehouse presents another example of dirt and muddle, and Krook himself is said to be known among the neighbours as 'the Lord Chancellor'.

Both the High Court of Chancery, at the summit of the legal system, and Tom-all-Alone's, the most miserable of slums, exhibit the same kind of decay. It is found equally in the world of fashion and aristocracy at Chesney Wold, the world of philanthropy represented by the follies of Mrs Jellyby and Mrs Pardiggle, and the world of shopkeepers and *petite bourgeoisie* represented by Krook and the Smallweeds. The world of art, represented by Skimpole, is characterised by his muddled homelife and constant debts, and religion does not come off any better with the hypocritical humbug of Chadband and the over-righteous harshness of Miss Barbary. Even the way parents bring up their children seems curiously flawed. Not only are there a number of orphans in the novel – Jo, Richard and Ada, Charley, Emma and Tom, Guster and the two young Smallweeds – but many of the parents fail to provide comfortable homes for their children – Mrs Jellyby, Mrs Pardiggle and old Mr Turveydrop, to give a few examples.

Many readers see *Bleak House* as an attack on the law and the High Court of Chancery, for causing all this decay and neglect, but even a brief survey of all the areas of dereliction in the novel suggest that *Bleak House* is about more than that. The novel is an indictment of the whole dark muddle of English society in the Victorian age, a muddle created, Dickens believed, by a monstrous apathy, irresponsibility and selfishness, of which the Court of Chancery, which was actually meant to protect people, stands as the most important symbol.

In Dickens's view, the decay, disease and neglect which characterised mid-Victorian society was due to a desperate lack of loving and caring responsibility, and that lack was felt everywhere. The High Court of Chancery, which had a special responsibility for the weak and infirm, does not care about its suitors; and Tom Jarndyce, Gridley, Miss Flite and Richard are all virtually destroyed by it. Nor does Chancery care for the poor wretches who live in the property it owns, such as Tom-all-Alone's, for the houses are terribly neglected, as we learn in Chapter 16. The aristocracy does not care about the poor, as Dickens's angry rhetoric – 'Dead, my lords and gentlemen' – emphasises in his account of Jo's death. Parliament is just a joke, indifferent to everything except its own survival, as the satire of Coodle and Doodle, and Buffy and Cuffy, and the pointed account of the General Election (in Chapter 40), makes quite clear. Philanthropy, as practised by Mrs Jellyby and Mrs Pardiggle, is often foolishly ineffective. With Skimpole's art only amateurish trifling, and Chadband's religion only hypocritical preaching, Dickens's confidence in the major social forces for goodness is thus almost non-existent. Even the love and responsibility parents are normally expected to feel for their children are frequently lacking, and few parents come well out of *Bleak House*.

Human beings do not live in isolation, completely separated from each other; as John Donne, the Jacobean poet and priest said, 'No man is an Iland, intire of itself; if a Clod be washed away by the Sea, Europe is the lesse', and he went on to say that 'any man's death diminishes me, because I am involved in Mankinde'. Dickens agrees passionately, believing that human beings are mutually dependent upon each other for love and support, however remote the connections between them may sometimes appear to be.

As the mysteries in *Bleak House* begin to be explained, so the connections between apparently unconnected and separate characters and events become clearer. The case of *Jarndyce* and *Jarndyce* in the High Court of Chancery has repercussions at Chesney Wold in Lincolnshire, which affect an illegitimate schoolgirl from Reading, and ultimately leads to the murder of a lawyer in London. Richard Carstone proves to be a distant relation of Sir Leicester, and Boythorn turns out to have been the suitor of Lady Dedlock's sister. Grandfather Smallweed's wife is discovered to be Krook's sister, and Esther finds that Mrs Chadband is her godmother's servant, Mrs Rachel. Most remarkable of all, Esther discovers her own unexpected relationship with Lady Dedlock.

Dickens makes this point about the unexpected interconnectedness of human relationships perfectly clear when in Chapter 16 he describes Sir Leicester Dedlock at Chesney Wold attended by a powdered footman (like the god Mercury), and then switches the narrative to London. 'What connexion can there be, between the place in Lincolnshire, the house in town, the Mercury in powder, and the whereabouts of Jo the outlaw with the broom,' he asks, and then continues, 'What connexion can there have been between many people in the innumerable histories of the world, who, from opposite sides of great gulfs, have, nevertheless, been very curiously brought together!'

Neglect or indifference to the network of human relationships, however, is always serious and sometimes can be tragic. The irresponsibility of the High Court of Chancery leads to the deaths of Tom Jarndyce, Gridley and Richard Carstone. Neglect of children by their parents can lead to disaster, as it does in the case of Lady Dedlock. And neglect of the disease-ridden slums of Tom-all-Alone's by the High Court of Chancery, and ultimately Parliament, can bring disease to St Albans and rural Lincolnshire. 'And therefore never send to know for whom the bell tolls,' says John Donne, 'It tolls for thee.' Human beings are mutually dependent upon each other, and selfish irresponsibility can have tragic consequences, even when it seems least likely.

Dickens's view of English society is, then, very bleak. He seems to have no faith in the Court of Chancery, in Parliament, the aristocracy, the Church, in art or philanthropy. Yet these are the very institutions which should care for the less fortunate members of society, to whom they are connected by all kinds of ties. (Significantly, Dickens links all these institutions together by associating them with images of fog, mud, darkness and dirt.) The novel ends in a whole series of defeats – with Lady Dedlock unreclaimed, with the Chancery case collapsing, and with Richard dying broken with disappointment.

Yet Dickens is not completely pessimistic. Though he does not, on the whole, believe in the value or efficiency of institutions, he is full of admiration for the integrity and goodness of those individuals who lead lives of loving and caring responsibility, often in circumstances which make their efforts truly heroic. Mr Jarndyce's generosity, Allan Woodcourt's steadfast help to Jo and Miss Flite, Trooper George and Phil Squod's kindness are all examples of individual responsibility; and it is characteristic of Dickens's genius that he saw loving responsibility flowering in the most trying circumstances and unlikely places. He sees it in the gifts harrassed Mr Snagsby and the frightened Guster make to Jo, in the way Caddy Jellyby takes on the burden of supporting her family, and in the way Mrs Bagnet sets out for Chesney Wold to try and prove Trooper George's innocence. Above all, Dickens sees it in the brave struggle Charley Neckett makes in Chapter 15 to look after her brother and sister when her father dies, and in the long heroic struggle of Esther to overcome all her setbacks and sense of inadequacy after her demoralising childhood. (Dickens links all these examples of loving responsibility by associating them with images of sunlight, cleanliness and order.)

Thus *Bleak House* ends not in complete disaster, but with a series of modest victories to set against the overall impression of defeat and decay. Charley Neckett survives to marry a miller, Caddy Jellyby prospers, and Esther and Allan have been happily settled for seven years as the novel ends. Though society's irresponsibility and selfishness are almost overwhelmingly destructive, it is possible for some loving and responsible individuals to achieve happiness, even in the most unpromising circumstances.

3.2 LAW AND LAWYERS

Though many of the other themes in *Bleak House* can be regarded as subordinate aspects of the central themes of responsibility and irresponsibility – the treatment of the law, of philanthropy and of family relationships, to give three examples – Dickens does have a good deal to say about them, which is worth considering in some detail. The High Court of Chancery and the way it deals with the case of *Jarndyce* and *Jarndyce* is not only a powerful symbol of irresponsibility, but its place in the novel also enables Dickens to discuss the law and the behaviour of lawyers in mid-Victorian England.

First of all, it is clear that the law and lawyers have a very important part to play in the novel. The action of *Bleak House* actually began years before the novel opens with the start of the Jarndyce case, and many other events in the story are indirectly concerned with legal matters, such as the birth of Esther, who is illegitimate. Many of the characters in the novel are employed as lawyers or lawyers' assistants, such as Tulkinghorn, Kenge and Carboy, Guppy, Jobling and Vholes. Even minor characters such as Detective Bucket, Nemo and Mr Snagsby indirectly depend on the law for their livelihood.

Yet the effect of the law is almost entirely destructive. It kills Tom Jarndyce, Gridley, Miss Flite's family and Richard Carstone, and does nothing to help Jo or Trooper George Rouncewell. The dilapidated slum, Tom-all-Alone's, 'is in Chancery, of course' (Chapter 16), but Chancery does nothing to help the miserable wretches who live there. The law, established to provide justice for all, and in the case of the High Court of Chancery especially set up to protect the rights of individuals, was so inordinately slow and so expensive that it brought misery instead of justice or mercy. Even in such early novels as *Pickwick Papers* and *Oliver Twist*, Dickens had treated the law-courts satirically, but his picture of the law in *Bleak House* is almost without hope.

The law is bad, Dickens says, because it has become an impersonal system which puts a higher value on orderly and consistent procedures, and on the perpetuation of self, than on the protection of human rights, which are its real responsibility. 'The one great principle of English law is, to make business for itself', Dickens says in Chapter 39, and justice has become a mere by-product of the law. Lawyers are an independent, self-perpetuating business-circle with their own closed society of rules and procedures. At its best the law is administered by people like Kenge and Guppy, who are absurd, and at its worst by people such as Tulkinghorn and Vholes who are wickedly inhuman. Lawyers care nothing for justice, but only for the law and money. Tulkinghorn is willing to use his legal power to bully Trooper George and to humiliate Lady Dedlock, while Vholes uses his to bleed Richard of every penny he can get. Mrs Bagnet speaks a bitter truth when she says of the innocent Trooper, 'It won't do to have the truth and justice on his side; he must have law and lawyers' (Chapter 55). It is a view Dickens endorses at almost every point.

3.3 CHARITY AND PHILANTHROPY

Another theme Dickens deals with in *Bleak House* is that of charity and philanthropy. Dickens himself was a tireless philanthropist who not only wrote regularly about social problems in his weekly magazines, but gave public readings from his novels to help raise money for working people, and also gave practical help to such projects as a slum-clearance scheme in Bethnal Green. To the surprise of many of Dickens's readers, however, *Bleak House* clearly satirises a number of would-be philanthropists, particularly Mrs Jellyby and her loquacious assistant, Mr Quale, with their scheme for settling colonists in Africa, and Mrs Pardiggle, a member of

the High Church Movement, whose religious sympathies do little to help
the poor brickmakers of St Albans, and who bullies her children into
giving their pocket-money to 'worthy' causes. Mr Chadband's unctuous
preaching at Jo is similarly satirised.

Dickens was not opposed to charity, but he believed that it should be
well conceived and of genuinely *practical* help. Mrs Jellyby's plans for
Borrioboola-Gha end disastrously, and Mrs Pardiggle's schemes are quite
ineffective. At the same time, both mothers make their own children
desperately unhappy! The true philanthropists in *Bleak House* are Mr
Jarndyce, Esther, Captain Hawdon, Mr Snagsby, Guster, Trooper George
and Phil Squod, who all help Jo. Mrs Bagnet helps George at a crucial
moment in the novel, and the efforts of Mrs Blinder and Mr Gridley to
help the Necketts should not be forgotten. There are perhaps questions
about Mr Jarndyce's self-effacing charity, however. Does not his toleration
of Skimpole and Mrs Jellyby contradict his attempts to help Jo and others
less fortunate? And is Mrs Jellyby's new-found concern for women's rights
in the last chapter another sign of folly or of improvement? Or does it tell
us more about Dickens's own feelings?

3.4 LOVE AND MARRIAGE

Though few readers think of *Bleak House* as a great love-story, there are,
in fact, many romantic liaisons and marriages in the novel, which are
treated by Dickens with a characteristic mixture of comedy and seriousness.
The marriages of Sir Leicester and Lady Dedlock, of the Snagsbys, the
Jellybys, the Bagnets, of Richard and Ada, and of Esther and Allan all
contribute to the discussion of love and marriage in *Bleak House*, and the
novel also depicts a number of people disappointed in love, such as Boythorn,
Miss Barbary and Guppy.

Dickens portrays a number of marriages which are unsuccessful for a
variety of reasons. The Jellyby marriage fails to work because Mrs Jellyby
ignores her husband, and the Snagsbys' marriage runs into difficulties
because of Mrs Snagsby's suspicious jealousy. Mr Bayham Badger's
marriage, on the other hand, seems absurd because he is willing to suffer a
total eclipse in favour of his wife's two previous husbands. Skimpole
simply behaves frivolously. Richard and Ada are the most conventionally
romantic couple in the novel, but their relationship is doomed because
Richard depends on the Chancery settlement too much, and refuses to
face responsibility. Sir Leicester and Lady Dedlock's marriage, on the
other hand, seems to be quite lifeless, until, faced by disaster, Sir Leicester
reveals how passionately he really cares for his wife.

Of the successful marriages in the novel, those of Caddy Jellyby and of the Bagnets seem best, though it is interesting that in both cases Dickens shows the wife as having to shoulder the greater responsibility. (Mr Bagnet never admits this, of course – 'I never own to it before the old girl. Discipline must be maintained.') Esther's developing relationship with Mr Jarndyce and Allan Woodcourt is the most interesting treatment of love in *Bleak House*, however. Torn between affectionate respect for her guardian and timidity about her real feelings, Esther patiently endures to achieve the most mature relationship in the novel.

3.5 PARENTS AND CHILDREN

In a novel which concentrates on the importance of human responsibility, it is not surprising to find so many parent-child relationships portrayed. All children automatically bestow a responsibility for their welfare upon their parents, and Dickens examines a wide variety of cases in the novel in order to see how effectively that responsibility is discharged.

On the whole, the world of *Bleak House* contains few loving parents and very few happy children. A number of children are orphaned and therefore subjected to an extremely harsh upbringing. Jo has no idea who his parents were. Guster came from a notorious orphanage-farm, and Phil Squod was found in the gutter and brought up by a violent tinker. Skimpole and Mrs Jellyby neglect their children, while Mrs Pardiggle ferociously bullies hers. In the Smallweed family the grandparents bring their orphaned grandchildren up to be prematurely old. Not only are Bart and Judy physically underdeveloped, but Judy, we are told, 'never owned a doll, never heard of Cinderella, never played at any game' (Chapter 21). Esther herself, though provided for in material ways, had an extremely unhappy childhood, brought up in guilt and shame by her aunt, Miss Barbary.

The only relationship between parents and children in the novel that shows normal family affection is that between Mr and Mrs Bagnet and their children, Quebec, Malta and young Woolwich. The other loving relationships tend to be those of surrogate or adopted parents, as when Charley Neckett becomes a loving parent to her younger brother and sister, or when Esther gradually becomes responsible for Ada and her guardian, Mr Jarndyce. In another extraordinary reversal of roles in the novel, Caddy Jellyby finds that she has to look after her father-in-law, old Mr Turveydrop, as if he were a child, as well as nursing her own deaf and dumb little girl.

Relationships between parents and children in *Bleak House*, then, tend to display the same lack of care and responsibility as dominates the rest of the novel. Ada's baby son Richard, and Esther's two little daughters, because of their loving parents, perhaps point to a more helpful future at the close.

4 TECHNICAL FEATURES

4.1 PLOT AND STRUCTURE

Like such novelists as Charlotte Brontë and Mrs Gaskell, Dickens used recent history rather than the remote past to give realism to the plots of his novels, and *Bleak House*'s picture of the ineffective workings of the Court of Chancery, where the celebrated Jennings case, begun in 1798, was still not settled in 1852, suggests that Dickens was dealing with very recent history indeed. References to slums and pollution were also extremely topical, for nearly 15 000 people died of cholera in 1849 in London alone. Even the jokes in Chapter 40 about Britain being without a government are based on real events in the early 1850s when the Prime Minister resigned and no one else could form a government for a fortnight! Dickens was clearly dealing with the problems of real life.

But Dickens's realism is not quite so straightforward as the presence of so many topical elements suggests, for in the Preface to the novel he significantly says, 'In *Bleak House* I have purposely dwelt upon the romantic side of familiar things.'

Many readers will have noticed that Esther's progress in the novel is a sort of Cinderalla story, about a lonely and unhappy orphan girl, brought up by a cruel stepmother figure until she is rescued by a fairy godfather (Jarndyce), with Allan Woodcourt appearing as a fairytale prince.

More important than the fairy-tale element, however, is the way Dickens exploits some of the devices we now recognise as typical of the detective story and suspense fiction, of which *Bleak House* is one of the earliest examples. The novel is full of mysteries, detectives and unexpected discoveries, and its plot focuses upon three major questions – about Lady Dedlock's secret past, the identity of Tulkinghorn's murderer, and the outcome of the Chancery case.

The first two aspects of the plot, the mysteries concerning Lady Dedlock and Tulkinghorn's murder, come closest to the form of the modern detective story. Indeed, in the fact that Lady Dedlock's story actually takes place before the novel opens, the crime of murder, and the use of a detective to carry out the investigations, *Bleak House* possesses some of the classic ingredients of the genre. Detectives, in fact, abound in the first two-thirds of the novel, for apart from the unforgettable Inspector Bucket, a great many other characters work at unravelling the novel's mysteries. Mr Tulkinghorn stalks Lady Dedlock's dark secret with menacing persistence; Mr Guppy, with his friend Weevle, tries to solve the mystery of Esther's identity; Krook, Guppy and the Smallweeds all furtively scrabble for Nemo's papers; and Bucket, Allan Woodcourt and even Mrs Bagnet become involved in the matter of Tulkinghorn's murder.

Dickens carefully structures the solutions to the various mysteries of his plots, so that when the secret of Esther's identity and Lady Dedlock's motherhood is solved in Chapter 36, he switches attention to the behaviour of Mr Tulkinghorn, who is murdered in Chapter 48. When that mystery is solved in Chapter 54, the detective elements in the novel are replaced by elements of the suspense story, and the reader is forced to speculate, not about what has happened and why, but about what will happen in the future. The reader's interest now focuses upon what will happen to the main characters, especially to Lady Dedlock now her secret is known, and to the young wards who have such great hopes of the Chancery settlement.

The novel does not deal with the three areas of mystery and suspense in a straightforward linear way, however, and even in the earlier parts of *Bleak House* incidents occur which relate to the matter of Tulkinghorn's murder or the outcome of the Chancery case, which will not come to a head until much later in the novel. Similarly there are events in the novel, such as Mr Jarndyce's conversation with Esther in Chapter 17, which help to explain and clarify events which happened in her childhood, as described in Chapter 3.

Since all or almost all the characters in the novel have some kind of connection with the High Court of Chancery, it might be best to visualise the structure of the novel not in the form of a geometrical diagram, as is possible with Jane Austen's *Pride and Prejudice*, or Thomas Hardy's *Jude the Obscure*, for example, but in the shape of a spider's web with Chancery at the centre. Thus the radiating theads link the different episodes and characters with Chancery, while other threads link these episodes with each other.

Chapter 2, for instance, concentrates upon the Dedlocks, but reveals their connection with the Jarndyce case, and also introduces the sinister lawyer, Tulkinghorn. Chapter 3 switches to the story of Esther, who is connected to Chancery through her relationship with the wards of court, but is also connected with the mystery of Lady Dedlock through her birth, although that is not to be revealed for some time. Chapter 5 continues the story of Esther, but her encounter with Krook and Miss Flite anticipates the disillusion of Richard's hopes at the end of the novel. Thus Dickens weaves and interweaves various strands from his three different, but interconnected, plots in a series of apparently disconnected episodes until the reader's detective work establishes the connections between them.

In addition to these characteristics of a detective story, *Bleak House* also makes use of such literary devices as parallelisms and thematic variations, so that the novel is full of minor characters and sub-plots. Richard's expectations of Chancery are paralleled by those of Miss Flite and Mr Gridley in the present, and by those of Tom Jarndyce in the past, while the disreputable rag and bottle merchant Krook is actually known as the Lord Chancellor by his cronies. The relationship between parents and children is another subject of frequent parallelisms in the novel, too, and in the sub-plots of Mrs Jellyby and Caddy, of the Bagnets, and of Trooper George and his mother, the reader is able to compare different examples of family life.

It is the presence of so many mysteries and so many detectives that gives *Bleak House* its particular flavour, however, and their function in the novel is very important indeed. By the end of the story the reader has discovered the secret of Lady Dedlock's past, the identity of Tulkinghorn's murderer, and the results of the Jarndyce case. More than that, however, Dickens uses his story to reveal a number of quite unexpected relationships. Not only does the reader discover that Lady Dedlock is Esther's mother and Captain Hawdon (alias Nemo) her father, but Miss Barbary, who brought up Esther, turns out to be Lady Dedlock's sister and also the woman Boythorn loved. Trooper George turns out to be the son of Mrs Rouncewell, the Dedlocks' housekeeper, and also the army friend of Captain Hawdon. Mrs Chadband is revealed as Esther's former nurse, Mrs Rachel; Mrs Bucket's lodger is found to be Hortense, and Krook turns out to be Mrs Smallweed's brother.

What Dickens is doing in *Bleak House*, in other words, is using a combination of detective story and suspense story to depict mysteries and their solutions, but, while it is true that *Bleak House* does contain a murder, the investigation of that murder and the desperate search for a missing person, the novel is equally concerned with establishing the true identities of, and the true relationships between, the main characters. The novel is not complete until the characters recognise themselves and their true relationships with each other. Esther does not find herself until she has discovered who her parents are. Sir Leicester cannot know how much he loves his wife until he has learned her history. Richard Carstone learns to recognise the truth about Mr Jarndyce and about Ada. Trooper George again becomes the son of Sir Leicester's housekeeper, and Mr and Mrs Snagsby become reconciled as man and wife. Finally, Esther discovers her true feelings about Mr Jarndyce – and about Allan Woodcourt.

Some readers find Dickens's use of coincidences unconvincing, and dislike the way the novel reveals so many unexpected relationships. Dickens was not working within the meticulously realistic tradition of Jane Austen's novels, however, but within the form of the newly-emerging detective and suspense story, where the plots frequently and inevitably consist of sudden revelations of surprising relationships. Dickens was trying to depict 'the romantic side of familiar things'. He also had a powerful sense of human brotherhood, and felt strongly about the ways men and women betray their responsibilities towards each other. The use of the techniques of the detective story with its sudden revelations about the past and about unexpected ties of blood and common humanity seems a perfect way of revealing human brotherhood and man's neglect of it.

4.2 NARRATIVE TECHNIQUE

The narrative technique which Dickens adopted for *Bleak House* was the unusual one of dual narrators. The novel is divided into 67 chapters, 34 told by an omniscient narrator who refers to events in the third person, and 33 chapters told by an autobiographical narrator, Esther, from her own, first-person point of view.

Such a technique is extremely unusual, but a comparison between these two kinds of narration reveals an amazing number of effects which they enabled Dickens to achieve. Those chapters using the third-person technique – such as Chapters 1, 2, 7 and 10, to begin with – present a wide and panoramic view of English society, sweeping from the High Court of Chancery in London up to Chesney Wold in Lincolnshire, then back again to London, to Mr Snagsby's premises, and then (briefly) to Paris and all over England again, from such places as Tom-all-Alone's to Lady Dedlock's mausoleum in Lincolnshire. The third-person narrative, we might say, enables Dickens to portray almost the whole of English society from the highest to the lowest, and he finds irresponsibility and cruelty everywhere.

Esther's narrative by comparison is much more modest. Esther herself is a very modest person, and in her story deals with a limited range of personal experiences, her own childhood, the meeting with Ada and Richard, and her life with Mr Jarndyce at Bleak House. She does travel, and she does meet other people, the Jellybys, Harold Skimpole, and eventually her own mother, but most of her encounters are of a domestic character, and she is often involved with families and young children, such as Caddy and Peepy, the Pardiggles, and the Necketts. Despite all her difficulties, Esther succeeds in achieving a modest degree of happiness by the end of the novel, as do Caddy and Charley, too, and in their individual successes Dickens may be deliberately making the point that, while the third-person panoramic view shows how England is suffering in general, it is possible for individuals of courage and responsibility to cope.

Another effect of the use of the two narrators is what the critic W. J. Harvey has called 'pulsation'. Esther's narrative tends to be calm and reasonable. It is the story of a shrewd and intelligent, but essentially un-flamboyant, observer, describing her relationships with a small group of friends in an unhurried manner. But after reading two or three chapters in this mode, the reader is switched to the third-person narration, where suddenly all is pace and movement as new characters and locations are in-troduced, often without any explanation, in ways that can be quite bewildering. The reader is thus offered expansion, pace and movement, and then suddenly finds contraction and stability in the first-person world of Esther Summerson. This contrast is one of the most distinctive features of *Bleak House*.

The way characters and places reappear in one of the narrative modes after appearing in the other also gives the novel one of its most striking dramatic effects, that has been likened to the *déjà vu* impression we some-times have when we see something and *feel* we have seen it before, although we *know* rationally that this is very unlikely. There are actually a number of straightforward examples of *déjà vu* in the novel such as when in Chapter 7 Guppy is reminded of someone when he sees Lady Dedlock's portrait but cannot connect this with meeting Esther earlier. Another example of this feeling of *déjà vu* occurs when Jo meets Hortense in Chapter 22 and confuses her with Lady Dedlock, whom he had met in Chapter 16.

It is also disconcerting, however, when a character first introduced in one narrative mode reappears in another. That happens with Mr Guppy in Chapter 7, and it happens more strikingly on other occasions in the novel. Allan Woodcourt, for example, first appears in the third-person story as the anonymous surgeon who attends to the dead Nemo in Chapter 11, so the reader meets him then, but Esther herself does not meet him until the dinner-party at the Bayham Badger's in Chapter 13. Similarly, Lady Dedlock features in the novel in the third-person narration from the second chapter, and Dickens achieves a remarkable effect when he describes Esther (but not the reader) seeing her for the very first time in Chesney Wold church in Chapter 18.

This *déjà vu* technique not only enables Dickens to surprise his readers and emphasise 'the romantic side of familiar things', but it is the cause of some of the most subtle effects in the novel, for it often enables him to describe an experience from two distinct points of view. Esther's response to Chesney Wold in Chapter 18 is quite different from the omniscient narrator's account in Chapter 2, for instance, and perhaps tells us something about Esther. It is also interesting that Guppy, who so often cuts a foolish figure in Esther's company, should prove to be quite resourceful when pursuing his investigation of Nemo, and this perhaps tells us something about Guppy. The most striking effect of the use of the two narrators occurs, however, in the dramatic account of the search for Lady Dedlock in Chapters 56–59, and what gives these chapters their particular intensity is the fact that they represent a convergence and concentration of energy when Bucket, a figure from the third-person narrative, joins Esther, the heroine of the first-person story.

The use of two narrative strands also enables Dickens to display a wonderful command of language, too. The style of the omniscient, third-person narrator is characteristically Dickensian in its richness. Always employing the present tense in such a way as to convey immediacy and urgency, the third-person narrator's range varies from the laconic use of sentence fragments and present participles in the opening description of the London fog to the eloquent but angry rhetoric with which Jo's death is announced. There is typically Dickensian energy and invention in the accounts of Chesney Wold, the slums of Tom-all-Alone's, the Coroner's inquest at the Sol's Arms, and Tulkinghorn's murder.

Esther seems to have a plainer, more subdued style. Dickens is using her as a normal person to act as a witness of the harm society inflicts upon individuals. She is truthful and independent, and corroborates Dickens's account of the way things are by being involved in them.

Thus her narrative style is personal and retrospective. She is looking back on events which took place at least seven years earlier, and, in doing so, through the stories of Richard and the Jellybys and the Necketts, she confirms the evidence of the third-person narrative. But within that account Esther describes her own modest successes, and some readers are irritated by this, feeling that somehow she is both modest and yet conceited, and therefore implausible. Such a reading is to miss Dickens's subtlety. Esther's narrative and her oscillations between apparent modesty and the need to report every word of love or praise given her, reflects the guilty, insecure personality which her upbringing as an illegitimate child of the Victorian Age has given her. It is typical of Dickens's psychological insight into Esther that her intelligence enables her to observe sharply the follies of Mrs Jellyby and the hypocrisies of Mr Skimpole, while her insecurities lead her to tread very warily in exposing them.

Both narrative forms also contain many literary elements characteristic of almost all Dickens's novels – symbolism, suspense, comedy, pathos, and the use of the grotesque especially.

Bleak House is particularly rich in dramatic suspense, from our interest in the young wards in the first chapter to the much greater mysteries involving Lady Dedlock, Esther's identity and Tulkinghorn's murder. Excitement carries right through to the close with the dramatic story of Lady Dedlock's flight and Bucket's breathless pursuit of her, and the great climax (or anticlimax) of the Chancery case.

The novel is also full of humour, with a host of comic characters and entertaining scenes, ranging from Guppy's proposals to Esther and his mother's indignation when she rejects him for the second time, to the extremist blusterings of Boythorn, the pride of Bayham Badger in his wife's former husbands, and of Mr Bagnet for Mrs Bagnet. Dickens's satire is also especially sharp in *Bleak House* and, as well as exposing the iniquities of Chancery and lawyers, comic attacks are also directed at the irresponsibility of Mrs Jellyby and Mrs Pardiggle, at old Mr Turveydrop's vanity about his deportment, at Chadband's oily sentiments, and the parliamentary inanities of Coodle and Doodle.

Dickens's handling of pathos does not always please his readers, for his language is sometimes excessively sentimental, but *Bleak House*, on the whole, shows a restraint which is often extremely effective. The treatment of the brickmakers, of Caddy Jellyby's baby, and of Charley Neckett looking after her younger brother and sister are all deeply poignant, while the death of Lady Dedlock and Sir Leicester's subsequent grief are handled with quiet dignity. Though some readers may find the description of Jo's death over-manipulative, few are unmoved by Dickens's angry denunciation at the end.

Different from the comic or sad is the way Dickens was able to describe certain incidents, places or people, so as to arouse a mixture of feelings of fear, fascination and even humour. These grotesque elements are particularly strong in *Bleak House*, and while Miss Flite and Mr Vholes have some of their characteristics, the strongest representatives are probably Krook and his extraordinary warehouse, and Grandfather Smallweed, who is like a spider spinning webs to catch unwary flies, yet also amuses the reader by the way he is constantly hurling cushions at his aged wife.

The name Smallweed, reminding the reader of a plant that never grows healthily, is typical of the way Dickens gives his characters names with symbolical associations, and Hawdon's pseudonym of Nemo is, of course, the most obvious example. The name of the Dedlocks reminds us of something that is metaphorically frustrated or frozen in some way, the name of Weevle is that of a kind of beetle, and Vholes that of a mouse-like rodent. Krook has clear associations with dishonesty, and other names hint at possible meanings, with Flite suggesting a half-wit, Barbary a barbarian or cruel person, and Trooper George an honest English soldier.

Symbolism extends well beyond names in *Bleak House*, however, and houses, for example, are often used to tell us something about their inhabitants, from Tom-all-Alone's and the brickmakers' cottages to Krook's warehouse, Tulkinghorn's chambers with Allegory on the ceiling, Chesney Wold with its Ghost's Walk, and Bleak House with its own ironical name. Birds, too – normally symbols of innocence and freedom – have several important references in the novel, treated with affection by Esther and Boythorn, imprisoned and then liberated by Miss Flite, and threatened by Krook's cat, Lady Jane. Krook's spontaneous combustion, too, may not satisfy the realists, but is a wonderfully poetic way of suggesting how the world of Chancery may end.

The great themes of *Bleak House* are, however, those of irresponsibility and selfishness, and of loving care and responsibility, and these contrasting themes are stamped with an almost Shakespearian richness of imagery and metaphor. Dickens had no faith in Chancery or the law, philanthropy or the Church, the *petite bourgeoisie* or the aristocracy, and he links their irresponsibility together with images of fog and mud, darkness and dirt, from the account of the London fog creeping into the law-courts in Chapter 1, to the smoke in Mrs Jellyby's home, the darkness in Tulkinghorn's chambers, the dirt in Krook's warehouse and the slum of Tom-all-Alone's. The shadow that hangs over Esther's childhood and that threatens the happiness of Richard and Ada as early as Chapter 14 is part of that same baleful imagery.

But, though loving responsibility is not to be found in institutions, it is Dickens's passionate belief that it is to be found in the lives of caring and unselfish individuals such as Mr Jarndyce, Caddy Jellyby, Charley Neckett and Trooper George, in the affection of the Bagnet family, and in the heroic life of Esther. Their values are suggested, in contrast with the fog-symbolism of irresponsibility, by images of sunlight, cleanliness and order. Caddy's improvement is shown when she starts learning housekeeping at Miss Flite's in Chapter 14; we first meet Charley when she returns from washing in Chapter 15; Trooper George's military ablutions are described in Chapter 26; and there is a vigorous account of Mrs Bagnet's washing-up in Chapter 27!

Mr Jarndyce is almost always described in terms of light from his first appearance in Chapter 6, and the light from his figure is emphasised remarkably in Chapter 44. Esther herself is the supreme figure of loving responsibility, of course, helping to make Mrs Jellyby's house a more comfortable home from the moment she arrives, and bringing love to Bleak House, to the brickmakers' cottages, and wherever she goes. It is no coincidence that her name is Summerson.

4.3 CHARACTERISATION

Dickens sets his characters clearly and directly before his readers, paying attention to the external details of a character's appearance, especially the face, the clothes and physical mannerisms. Though in some of the novels he also attempts internal analysis of a person's thoughts, feelings and motivation, generally Dickens prefers to reveal a character through the way he looks and behaves, and particularly through the way he or she speaks. He is marvellously alert to little physical mannerisms and ways of speaking, and we get to know Dickens's characters from their behaviour over a long period of time rather than by the author's telling us all about them on their first appearance. When we first meet Sir Leicester in Chapter 2, for example, Dickens describes his physical appearance and his pride in the family name, and draws attention to the nature of his relationship with his wife by the way he always refers to her as 'My Lady', Later events help us to reach a fuller understanding of Sir Leicester's pride and of his relationship with his wife.

Dickens presents his characters with varying degrees of complexity – they are not given equal treatment of space. In a famous formulation, the author E. M. Forster, in *Aspects of the Novel*, tried to distinguish between characters presented with some degree of complexity, which he called 'round', and those presented as 'flat' characters, which are constructed round a single idea or quality. In *Bleak House*, for example, we might say that old Mr Turveydrop is a 'flat' character, distinguished only by a vain obsession with his 'deportment' which verges on monomania, while other characters, such as Sir Leicester, are more complicated and hence 'round' characters. Forster's suggestion has led to misunderstandings, however, and induced some readers to underestimate Dickens's powers of characterisation, because of the frequency with which he uses 'flat' characters. Nearly all literature presents characters who are developed in very varying degrees; even in Shakespeare's greatest plays minor characters such as Pistol and Bardolph lack the richness of Falstaff. Even minor, apparently 'flat' characters may also have an important functional role in the novel, as old Mr Turveydrop illustrates Dickens's major theme, that of irresponsibility. 'Flat' characters may also be rather more complicated than a simple stereotyping formula might suggest. Does not Mr Turveydrop's vanity, for example, tell us a good deal about the kind of society in which he grew up?

One of the most important aspects of Dickens's characterisation is the way he shows characters developing as the story proceeds. He takes a dynamic view of personality, in other words, and though some characters, such as old Mr Turveydrop, may not develop very much, others do so remarkably. *Bleak House* concentrates upon the changes in Esther and Richard primarily, but Caddy Jellyby, Trooper George, Sir Leicester and even Mrs Snagsby show some changes before the novel ends.

Ada Clare

Ada Clare has rich golden hair, soft blue eyes and an innocent and trusting nature. Her surname suggests that she is clear and free from impurities, and so indeed she proves.

An orphan and ward of the Court of Chancery in the Jarndyce case, she is placed in the care of John Jarndyce along with her distant cousin, Richard Carstone, and with Esther Summerson as her companion. She happily accepts Mr Jarndyce's protection and soon becomes Esther's dearest friend.

Ada's main relationship in *Bleak House*, however, is with Richard, and Esther notices that she is falling in love with him as early as Chapter 9. She loyally supports Richard in his difficulties over choosing a career, even when he decides to study law and she suspects that this worries Mr Jarndyce. Though saddened, she accepts Mr Jarndyce's advice to break off her engagement to Richard, and later writes a letter warning Richard against becoming too involved in the Chancery suit and turning against Mr Jarndyce. Her love continues, despite the gradual decline in Richard's fortunes, and she offers him her own small inheritance when he has money problems in the army.

When Esther is nursing Caddy Jellyby, Ada, who is just twenty-one, begins to reveal the tension created by her love for Richard and her affection for Mr Jarndyce. Esther also notices that she sleeps with one hand hidden under her pillow. Then Ada reveals that she and Richard have been secretly married for two months, and she joins him in his lodgings in Symond's Inn. Though Richard's decline continues, Ada never falters in her support, but she worries about the future and fears that Richard may not live to see the child she is bearing.

When the Chancery case ends and the crash of Richard's hopes kills him, he dies in Ada's arms begging her forgiveness. Later Ada has a baby boy she names after his father, and when the novel ends she is living in quiet contentment with her guardian, John Jarndyce. Though some readers have found Ada's unswerving goodness implausible, it acts as a good foil to Esther's more positive but more complicated personality.

Richard Carstone

Richard Carstone is a handsome young man, with an ingenuous face and most engaging laugh, when we first meet him. An orphan and ward of the court, like his cousin Ada, he is about nineteen, two years older than her. When they go to live with their guardian, Mr Jarndyce, Richard and Ada soon fall in love, and their future seems full of promise.

Richard is careless about money, however, and this weakness is accompanied by an indecisiveness of character. Esther believes that this may be due to his public-school education, but Mr Jarndyce believes that it may have been caused by Chancery's confirming in him a habit of putting off decisions, of trusting to chance.

Thus Richard first decides to make his career as a surgeon, but soon gives this up and turns to the study of law, thinking this will enable him to keep an eye on his prospects in the Jarndyce case, in which he has a claim. Despite his guardian's warnings not to place any hopes in it, he spends an increasing amount of time and energy in his suit and begins to get into debt.

When he changes his career again, and joins the army, he resents Mr Jarndyce's advice that he should end his engagement with Ada for the time being, and an estrangement grows up between them which is exacerbated when Richard declares his suspicion that Jarndyce has his own interests in the outcome of the Chancery case.

Richard continues to love Ada and Esther, but neither can dissuade him from his increasing involvement with the Court of Chancery. He employs the sinister Vholes as his legal adviser, and the Jarndyce affair takes such a hold on his nature that he begins to deteriorate physically. Comparing him with Krook, Weevle describes him as a case of 'smouldering combustion' (Chapter 39).

Richard leaves the army and marries Ada, but his decline continues as his haggard and slovenly appearance makes clear.

Allan Woodcourt befriends him in the latter stages of the novel, and his unselfish work as a doctor of the poor contrasts strongly with Richard's unstable character. Richard's heart is broken by the way the Chancery case ends, but reconciled with Mr Jarndyce, and asking Ada's forgiveness, he dies in her arms, poignantly planning to 'begin the world'.

Lady Dedlock

Twenty years younger than her husband, Lady Dedlock is in her mid-forties, and has a fine face and elegant figure. She is an admired leader in the world of fashion, and usually carries herself in a proud and apparently bored way. Her 'fatigued manner, and insolent grace' (Chapter 12) is what readers first notice about her.

There are several signs that Lady Dedlock is less composed than she appears, however. Even in Chapter 2, when Dickens emphasises Lady Dedlock's appearance of boredom, he draws the reader's attention to her interest in a child in the park, and Lady Dedlock is very disconcerted later when she recognises some legal handwriting. Her befriending of the new maid, Rosa, similarly implies a warmer, emotional side to her character.

Lady Dedlock has a secret past. Before she married Sir Leicester, she was in love with Captain Hawdon, by whom she had an illegitimate child, who she believed died at birth, though her elder sister, Miss Barbary, had in fact reared the baby in secrecy. Now married to Sir Leicester, Lady Dedlock longs to know what happened to Hawdon, and is amazed to discover that her child is still alive.

As her story is gradually revealed by the death of Nemo and the discoveries of Tulkinghorn, Lady Dedlock visits the places associated with her dead lover, and tries to make her peace with her daughter, now identified as Esther.

But Tulkinghorn, Sir Leicester's family lawyer, turns his discoveries about her past against Lady Dedlock. He threatens to expose her secret to her husband, and torments her with his power over her. Lady Dedlock's graceful self-possession breaks down. When Tulkinghorn is murdered, and Bucket's investigations lead to his exposing Lady Dedlock's past to her husband, she is thoroughly broken. Regretting the pain and disgrace she has brought Sir Leicester, she flees the home. Exhausted by her wanderings, she writes a farewell note to Esther begging her forgiveness and dies on the steps of the burial-ground where Captain Hawdon lies buried. It is one of the many ironies of *Bleak House* when Grandfather Smallweed reveals that the disgraced woman's christian name was Honoria (Chapter 54).

Sir Leicester Dedlock

Sir Leicester Dedlock is a handsome gentleman in his late sixties, with light grey hair and whiskers, who walks a little stiffly because he suffers from gout. A baronet, he is intensely conscious of his rank and proud of his family name. He acts as host to many distinguished guests and relatives at his residences in Chesney Wold and in London.

'Intensely prejudiced' and 'perfectly unreasonable', as Dickens describes him (Chapter 2), Sir Leicester quarrels violently with Boythorn over the right of way over his land. He is, moreover, particularly alarmed by Ironmaster Rouncewell's desire to have his wife's maid, Rosa, receive a better education than that provided by the village school. Sir Leicester is a dyed-in-the-wool representative of the old, landed, ruling class, in fact, and fears any attempt at change will lead to the floodgates of society being burst open! (The name Dedlock reminds us of something immovable, of course.)

But though Dickens criticises Sir Leicester as a reactionary representative of an irresponsible and selfish ruling class, and neatly exposes his corrupt electioneering in Chapter 40, he also praises some of his qualities as an individual. He is a kind master, well liked by his housekeeper and by Trooper George, courteous towards Rouncewell despite their differences, and also towards Mr Jarndyce later. Above all, he worships his wife, whom he treats with a stately gallantry, and usually refers to as 'My Lady'.

In the great crisis he behaves magnificently. Deeply upset when Bucket reveals his wife's secret past, he seems to have a stroke. Though he honours his family name profoundly, he puts love and compassion for his wife first, insisting that his relationship with her remains unchanged. His fidelity to his wife and conquest of his own pride for her sake are particularly moving because they are so unexpected.

Sir Leicester's career ends quietly with sad visits to his wife's mausoleum, accompanied by his faithful servant, George, and readings in the evenings by cousin Volumnia. The greater part of the house is shut up, and it is hard not to feel that Dickens is symbolising the decline of the social class Sir Leicester represents.

John Jarndyce

John Jarndyce is an upright, handsome man, with silvery grey hair, and aged about sixty. Bleak House's pleasant but delightfully irregular character mirrors his warm but slightly eccentric personality.

He is a genuine philanthropist, and not only accepts responsibility for the young wards Ada and Richard, but also looks after Esther, and has done so since her aunt died. He also tries to help other people, such as Mrs Jellyby, Harold Skimpole, the Necketts and Allan Woodcourt. In some ways he seems almost a symbol of benevolence.

But he is more complicated than that. Embarrassed by expressions of gratitude, he also dislikes news of cruelty in any form, pretending his discomfort is caused by the east wind! When he is deceived or disappointed by people, he takes refuge in the room he calls the Growlery.

He is particularly hostile to the Court of Chancery and any expectation of wealth arising from the Jarndyce case. He saw this ruin his great uncle Tom Jarndyce, who first named the house Bleak House, and consistently denounces entanglements with the law which he calls Wiglomeration. Thus, while he is willing to give Richard every help over his choice of a career, he consistently warns him against relying on a successful outcome of the Jarndyce case. Though this causes a break between them, they are reconciled before Richard dies.

From early on in the novel, Mr Jarndyce puts a high value on Esther's qualities, entrusting her with the housekeeping keys, and calling her Little Old Woman and other motherly names. Deeply sympathetic to her personal problems, he proposes to her by letter in Chapter 44, partly to protect her after her illness and the distress caused by her discovery of her past. When Allan Woodcourt returns from overseas, however, Mr Jarndyce realises that Esther really loves him, and unselfishly releases her to marry Woodcourt.

Some readers find Mr Jarndyce's proposed marriage to Esther an uncomfortable idea, but that may be Dickens's deliberate intention. He certainly raises questions about Jarndyce's naïveté in trusting Skimpole for so long.

Esther Summerson

Esther is the most interesting but also the most controversial character in the novel. Some readers find that the picture she paints of herself is too good to be true; others are irritated by her apparent modesty combined with the way she is always quoting other people's praise of her.

The clue to Esther's character lies in the circumstances of her birth and early childhood, however. The illegitimate daughter of Captain Hawdon and Lady Dedlock, with all the shame illegitimacy brought in the Victorian age, she was taken away from her mother at birth and brought up as an orphan in the sternly repressive atmosphere created by Lady Dedlock's sister, Miss Barbary. 'Your mother, Esther, is your disgrace, and you were hers,' she is told. 'You are different from other children. . .you are set apart' (Chapter 3).

Esther's inheritance of guilt and shame makes her try to become industrious and to do good, but, although she has some sense of innocence, she is usually dominated by feelings of inadequacy. Thus she is extremely shrewd about people, and gives vivid accounts of such characters as Mrs Jellyby and Skimpole, but she is usually reluctant to criticise them directly, as if unsure of her judgements. It is this insecurity which leads her to quote the compliments other people pay her; she desperately needs love, yet finds it hard to believe that she is worthy of it because of her upbringing.

Esther is of enormous practical help to everyone she meets. She brings some order to the Jellyby household, proves a loyal friend to Ada and Richard, and does her best for Jo and the Necketts. It is significant that while Ada weeps for the brickmaker's dead baby, it is Esther who takes it and gently covers it with her handkerchief. Mr Jarndyce recognises Esther's practical virtues when he gives her the housekeeping keys of Bleak House, a symbol of her responsibility.

But Esther's personality is not a static one. On the night she visits the sick Jo and catches the disease which will eventually lead to her reunion with her mother, she has a profound impression of her changing character. The dreams she has during her illness, however, symbolise her continuing guilt until the encounter with Lady Dedlock makes her realise, 'I was as innocent of my birth as a queen of hers' (Chapter 36).

She cannot completely rid herself of her lack of self-esteem, however – she is after all still a very young woman – and accepts Jarndyce's proposal of marriage out of a sense of gratitude, though her tears show where her real love lies. Fortunately Mr Jarndyce enables Esther to marry Allan Woodcourt at the end.

To sum up, Esther is not meant to be a conventionally attractive heroine from the beginning of the novel – she has considerable psychological problems – and we are not meant necessarily to rejoice in her company, as we might, say, with Jane Austen's Elizabeth Bennet or Shakespeare's Beatrice. But Esther is the supreme example in *Bleak House* of the way society disfigures and almost destroys individuals, but she also shows how they can sometimes attain happiness by heroically exercising love and responsibility.

Mr Tulkinghorn

Mr Tulkinghorn is an elderly, old-fashioned solicitor of the High Court of

Chancery, and legal adviser of the Dedlocks, who have an interest in the Jarndyce case. He usually wears black clothes and knee-breeches. A man who knows many legal secrets, he is intensely discreet about them, like 'an oyster of the old school' (Chapter 10).

He lives in a set of chambers in Lincoln's Inn Fields, and his physical surroundings mirror his character, for his apartment is lit by two candles only, a thick carpet muffles the floor, and there are very few papers left out for visitors to read. The painted figure of Allegory looks enigmatically down from his ceiling.

After noticing the way Lady Dedlock reacts to the handwriting on a legal document, Tulkinghorn gradually unearths the whole story of her relationship with Captain Hawdon. By revealing that he knows her secret, and by threatening to expose it to her husband, he causes Lady Dedlock great distress, which he deliberately prolongs by refusing to reveal exactly when he will tell Sir Leicester.

Mr Tulkinghorn represents evil, in other words, but the question arises as to what motivates his behaviour, since there seems to be no suggestion of his blackmailing Lady Dedlock for money. She comes, in fact, closest to understanding Tulkinghorn of anyone in the novel when she says, 'His calling is the acquisition of secrets and the holding of such power as they give him' (Chapter 36).

He is a lonely man whose only pleasure in life seems to be an enjoyment of old port. But, being a lawyer, he understands how the society of *Bleak House* works, and is extremely skilful at manipulating it. Thus he exploits Snagsby and Jo, Hortense and Trooper George for his purposes.

What he really enjoys is the power his knowledge gives him over people. We also know that he does not particularly like women – 'These women were created to give trouble the world over,' he says in Chapter 42. He takes a special pleasure in pursuing the beautiful and composed Lady Dedlock and it may be that her humilation gives him a peculiar kind of sexual satisfaction. It is, therefore, particularly appropriate that Hortense, a figure of open passion, should be responsible for his death. Humiliated by Tulkinghorn as Lady Dedlock was, she has enough energy to react against his repressed, manipulative personality.

Allan Woodcourt

Allan Woodcourt is the dark, young surgeon who attends the dead Nemo, and suggests there had been something in his manner which denoted a fall in life. He reappears at the dinner party given by the Bayham Badgers for Richard Carstone, meets Esther, and moves across from the third-person narrative to her autobiographical chapters. He plays a small but important part in the plot, befriending Richard, bringing the news of Tulkinghorn's murder, and forming the loving relationship with Esther which eventually leads to their marriage.

A surgeon, particularly concerned for the poor, Allan also functions as a figure of caring responsibility in the novel, and contrasts sharply with the irresponsible behaviour of Richard. He befriends and helps such unfortunates as Nemo, Miss Flite, Jo and Jenny, the brickmaker's wife. He tries to bring comfort to Richard as he sinks further into misery. The reader is not surprised to learn that Allan behaved like a hero when shipwrecked in the East Indies; his life is devoted to dealing with the victims of shipwrecks, metaphorically as well as literally.

His love-affair with Esther is delicately revealed with the first reticent reference in Chapter 13 and the account of his gift of flowers later. He exhibits a gentle commiseration for Esther's changed appearance in Chapter 45, and gradually moves closer to her. He behaves honourably when Esther explains why she is unable to marry him, and joyfully claims her when she is free. It is appropriate that he and Esther should go together to help the poor in Yorkshire at the end of the novel. In this way they can continue to alleviate pain and soothe the unfortunate.

Allan Woodcourt's mother, a pretty old lady with bright, black eyes, is immensely proud of her distinguished Welsh ancestry, and talks so much about it to discourage Esther from thinking she might be good enough to marry her son. She also tells Esther of Allan's flirtations in the hope that this will discourage her from thinking of him seriously. Gradually, with Mr Jarndyce's help, she softens towards Esther, however. In many ways she is not unlike Mr Guppy's mother, with her passionate interest in her son's choice of a wife. Indeed she is one of many parents whose treatment of their children is discussed in the novel.

Mr and Mrs Bagnet

The Bagnets are a military, or rather ex-military, family and it is therefore appropriate that their name is the old word for the military weapon, the bayonet. Matthew Bagnet is a tall, upright, ex-artillery man, with shaggy eyebrows and whiskers. Called Lignum because his tough face resembles the dense hardwood, he runs a shop selling musical instruments in the Elephant and Castle district of London. He plays the bassoon and his deep voice sounds like one. Mrs Bagnet is a large-boned, soldierly-looking woman aged between forty-five and fifty, with bright eyes and freckles, and is known to her husband as 'the old girl'. Their children are usually referred to by the names of the army barracks in which they were born: Quebec, Malta and Woolwich!

The Bagnets provide a good deal of humour in the novel – in the account of Mrs Bagnet's birthday party in Chapter 49, for example – but they also make important contributions to the plot and thematic interests of *Bleak House*.

Trooper George turns to them for advice when he is pressed by Tulkinghorn for a sample of Captain Hawdon's writing, and it is because he cannot let down Matthew Bagnet, who has stood surety for his loan, that George eventually gives the lawyer Hawdon's letter. When George is arrested for Tulkinghorn's murder, Mrs Bagnet travels to Lincolnshire to bring Mrs Rouncewell to urge him to use a lawyer, and so reunites a mother and lost child in the sub-plot in a way which parallels the reunion of Lady Dedlock and Esther in the main plot.

The Bagnets emerge as the most impressive family in the whole novel. Where other parents neglect or ill-treat their children, they positively celebrate family life. Though far from well off, their home is clean and the children well-fed, and, though their efforts make her uneasy, the family's preparations for Mrs Bagnet's birthday dinner illustrate the love and harmony in one household at least.

Mrs Bagnet is one of the major examples of responsibility in the novel, in fact. She looks after her husband and children capably, is a good friend of George, not afraid to criticise him for thoughtlessness but quick to forgive him too, and to help him when he gets into serious trouble. She is, in Trooper George's own words, 'as fresh and wholesome as a ripe apple on a tree' (Chapter 34). It is not surprising that Mr Bagnet thinks so highly of his wife, relying on *her* wisdom to give *him* advice, though he will never admit it in front of her, because, as he puts it, 'Discipline must be maintained' (Chapter 27).

Lawrence Boythorn

Lawrence Boythorn is a handsome old gentleman of about seventy, a man capable of fierce denunciations and then of roaring with laughter and displaying tenderness. His name is indeed a clue to his character, for it suggests the freshness of youth combined with the prickliness of a thorn.

He is a man of passionate feelings, particularly about the violation of principles. He rescued Mr Jarndyce from being bullied at school, and is in fierce controversy with Sir Leicester Dedlock concerning a disputed right of way over his property at Chesney Wold. He thus makes a striking contrast with Skimpole, and it is significant that they argue, not only about Sir Leicester's patronising behaviour but also because Boythorn believes in principles and Skimpole does not.

Boythorn always acts in extremes, however, chopping down Sir Leicester's gate, squirting water from a fire-engine over his servant, and even asserting that a coachman should be put to death for being twenty-five minutes late!

There are signs that his passionate nature may have caused him unhappiness, for Mr Jarndyce reveals that Boythorn was all but married to Lady Dedlock's sister, Miss Barbary, but she broke off the relationship after Esther was born, because, Mr Jarndyce says, of her knowledge of Boythorn's proud temper and his strained sense of honour.

Boythorn also shows gentleness and generosity, however. He makes his house available for Esther's convalescence, and always speaks of Lady Dedlock with sympathetic courtesy. After her death, he tries to abandon the dispute over the right of way, but Sir Leicester refuses, and Boythorn keeps it up, though 'it is whispered that when he is most ferocious towards his old foe, he is really most considerate' (Chapter 66). Boythorn's fondness for his canary, in a novel where birds are normally symbols of innocence, also reveals more of his passionate, complicated character.

Inspector Bucket

'Inspector Bucket of the Detective' is a stoutly-built, middle-aged man, with little remarkable about his appearance except the way he uses his fat forefinger for emphasis, and that he wears a mourning-ring on his little finger and a brooch in his shirt.

He is an accomplished professional policeman, and displays considerable skill and energy, both in the way he discovers the identity of Tulkinghorn's murderer, and in the search for Lady Dedlock. A sharp-eyed observer, he is an extremely shrewd interviewer, often flattering people to win their confidence, and doing so very successfully with Sir Leicester's servant, for example. He disguises himself skilfully in order to arrest Gridley, and deals firmly but discreetly with the blackmailing attempts of Grandfather Smallweed and the Chadbands.

Inspector Bucket also shows himself to be a person of some humanity. He tries to be as kind as possible when carrying out his official duties, consoling Gridley, being convivial with the Bagnets, and showing great consideration towards Esther. He recognises George's sterling qualities and takes the opportunity to tell his distressed mother of George's release from prison.

In presenting Bucket as a kindly but impersonal instrument of the law, however, Dickens does raise some disturbing questions about him. There is ambiguity about some of his actions, for example, and readers may wonder whether there is not an element of hypocrisy about his behaviour at the Bagnets. The way he moves Jo on (to his death) in order to avoid embarrassing the Dedlocks and Tulkinghorn is even more questionable. In a novel which exposes the law as frequently cruel and unjust, as in its treatment of Gridley, those who enforce the law cannot emerge untarnished. Mr Bucket seems to work only for Mr Tulkinghorn and Sir Leicester, and the reader may wonder why the detective could not be employed using his skills to track down the persons responsible for the diseases spread by the slum of Tom-all-Alone's.

Mr and Mrs Chadband

The Chadbands are religious hypocrites, and play small but important parts in *Bleak House*, contributing to the development of the plot and adding to the gallery of irresponsible characters.

Mrs Chadband first appears in Chapter 3 as Mrs Rachel, the servant of Miss Barbary, who helped to look after the young Esther. She reappears in the novel, married to Mr Chadband, at the Snagsby's afternoon-tea in Chapter 19. When the tea is interrupted by the arrival of a constable with Jo, Guppy identifies Mrs Chadband as Esther's former companion, and so takes up the trail of Lady Dedlock's past. Mrs Chadband is a stern, severe-looking woman, and her cold attitude towards Esther illustrates the austere treatment many people thought appropriate for illegitimate children in the Victorian age.

Mr Chadband, by contrast is 'a large yellow man, with a fat smile, and a general appearance of having a good deal of train oil in his system' (Chapter 19). He perspires heavily, and frequently has to wipe the oily exudation from his forehead with a flabby paw.

A clergyman, but belonging to no particular denomination, Chadband has a large following among such people as Mrs Snagsby, who particularly admires his style of preaching. His speech is, in fact, extremely pompous, full of platitudes and rhetorical questions which read hilariously. 'What is peace? Is it war? No. Is it strife? No,' he foolishly twitters in Chapter 19.

Though professing to be a Christian, however, Chadband shows little real charity. While eating prodigiously himself, he offers the starving Jo a religious discourse instead of food, and later blames Jo's orphaned and poverty-stricken state on his lack of 'Terewth.' Even worse, the Chadbands try to blackmail Sir Leicester, demanding money to keep quiet about his wife's secrets. It is not surprising that the name Chadband has become a synonym for an unctuous hypocrite.

Miss Flite

Miss Flite is a little old woman who usually carries a reticule containing some litter she calls her documents. Her strange talk and eccentric behaviour make her one of the most remarkable characters in the novel.

She has a minor but important part in the plot. She introduces Esther and the wards to Krook, fetches Allan Woodcourt to Nemo's deathbed, and reveals that a veiled lady took Esther's handkerchief from the brick-maker's cottage. She is a good friend to Caddy, to Esther – whom she walks twenty miles to visit when the girl is sick, to Gridley and to the dying Jo.

More importantly, however, like Tom Jarndyce, Gridley and Richard Carstone, she is a victim of Chancery and represents its destructive powers most vividly. What we first notice about Miss Flite is her demented behaviour – her name suggests someone flighty or silly – for that is what Chancery has done to her. She attends the court regularly, telling everyone, 'I expect a judgement shortly. On the day of Judgement' (Chapter 3).

She lives very poorly but keeps a large collection of birds in her room, to which she has given such unusual names as Ashes and Spinach.

Later the reader learns how her father, brother and sister all expected favourable judgements from Chancery, and all died disappointed. Miss Flite herself fell ill and when she recovered found that she too was drawn to the Court. 'You *can't* leave it. And you *must* expect,' she tells Esther (Chapter 35).

The names of her birds are symbolical, of course. They suggest Chancery's *victims* - Hope, Joy, Youth, Peace, Rest, Life; its *methods* - Cunning, Folly, Words, Wigs, Rags, Sheepskins, Plunder, Precedent, Jargon, Gammon and Spinach (i.e. nonsensical legal jargon); and its *results* - Dust, Ashes, Waste, Want, Ruin, Despair, Madness and Death.

Miss Flite soon recognises Richard's obsession with his Chancery case, and adds the wards in *Jarndyce* and *Jarndyce* to her collection of birds. When the case collapses and Richard dies, she comes weeping to say that she has given her birds their liberty. It is a tribute to her endurance that, though crazed by what she has suffered, she never completely loses her kindly humanity.

Mr Guppy

William Guppy is a young clerk who works for the lawyers Kenge and Carboy of Lincoln's Inn, and lives with his mother in Old Street Road. A minor and essentially comic figure, Guppy is a good example of the way Dickens employs a character for a variety of purposes.

Guppy first meets Esther in Chapter 4 when he escorts her and the wards to the Jellybys, but later, when visiting Chesney Wold, he notices a striking resemblance between Lady Dedlock's portrait and Esther. When he hears Jo's story of the veiled lady, and learns of Esther's childhood from Mrs Chadband, he carries out some clever detective work, which leads him to connect Lady Dedlock with Esther and Captain Hawdon. Though he fails to secure Hawdon's letters from Krook, he warns Lady Dedlock that others may use them against her, and so precipitates her flight. He thus adds a good deal to the action of the novel by his brilliant discoveries.

His main reason for making them is, of course, his romantic attachment to Esther, to whom he proposes in Chapter 9, and whom he pursues to theatres in absurd and embarrassing ways later. What makes Guppy's behaviour particularly comical is his language, which is ridiculously pompous at times, especially when he proposes to Esther. Less happily, Guppy insists that his proposal has been withdrawn when he realises Esther's face has been disfigured by her illness, though his use of legal jargon still gives even that scene a comic flavour.

Guppy, in fact, tends to seem a more absurd figure in Esther's story than in the third-person narrative, where he often displays energy and resourcefulness. He stands up for himself quite firmly against Mr Tulkinghorn, for instance, in Chapter 39. Perhaps his feeling for Esther makes him too self-conscious? At any rate, his passion for her contributes to the discussion of love affairs in the novel, as his protective but embarrassed relationship with his mother adds to the gallery of children and parents in *Bleak House*.

Mrs Jellyby, Mrs Pardiggle and the Turveydrops

Mrs Jellyby, Mrs Pardiggle and the Turveydrop family all make an important contribution to *Bleak House*, not only by providing comic relief but also because of the ways they help illustrate the themes of responsibility and irresponsibility in the novel, particularly in parent-child relationships.

A pretty, plump woman of between forty and fifty, Mrs Jellyby devotes herself almost entirely to public concerns, immersing herself in voluminous correspondence about African affairs, but neglecting her family in the process. Peepy gets his head stuck in railings, her house is full of crumbs, dust and waste paper, and the meals are not prepared properly; but Mrs Jellyby is unaware of all this. More importantly, she is unaware of her own children's unhappiness or her husband's bankruptcy, and receives the news of Caddy's marriage with indifference because she is so preoccupied with her African affairs. She is an example of what Dickens calls 'Telescopic Philanthropy' (Chapter 4) because she can only see the good that needs doing a long distance away.

Though treated more sketchily, Mrs Pardiggle is similar. A formidable lady with spectacles, a prominent nose and a loud voice, she is a tireless worker on behalf of numerous charities, but again lacks sensitivity. Under pressure from Mrs Pardiggle, her five young boys donate their pocket-money to various good causes, an act of forced charity which has made them so unruly they even pinch Esther! The names Mrs Pardiggle has given her children, all saints or heroes admired by the High Church (Puseyite) Movement of the 1840s, and the fact that she offers the poor brickmakers a book and preaching, suggest that Dickens is here satirising those Christians more concerned with creeds and sermons than with giving practical help.

Old Mr Turveydrop is irresponsible in a different kind of way. A fat old gentleman 'with a false complexion, false teeth, false whiskers, and a wig' (Chapter 14), he is a vain and idle fake. Immensely proud of his deportment, he allowed his wife to work herself to death in order to allow him to display himself in the fashionable world; and, while Prince runs the Dance Academy, teaching the pupils, playing the fiddle, dancing and playing the piano, his father stands before the fire, a model of deportment, patronising the son who works twelve hours a day to support him!

Caddy Jellyby makes a striking contrast to all these irresponsible parents. Determined to improve herself after first meeting Esther, she began taking dancing lessons and so met Prince. Falling in love with the little, blue-eyed man with flaxen hair, she marries him (with some help from Esther) and proceeds to become a model wife and mother. When her husband's health fails, she learns to give dancing lessons herself, and contrives to keep the peace between her mother and her father-in-law. She becomes a good mother to her own deaf and dumb child, and continues to smile and prosper despite all her difficulties.

She makes remarkable progress from the jaded, unhealthy and desperately unhappy child we meet at the beginning of the novel – and her development, despite all the difficulties in her way, is a sharp contrast to the irresponsibility of Mrs Jellyby, Mrs Pardiggle and Old Mr Turveydrop.

Mr Krook

Krook is one of Dickens's most sinister and extraordinary creations. A short and withered old man – aged seventy-six, we learn in Chapter 34 – he wears spectacles and a furry cap, and his throat, chin and eyebrows are frosted with white hairs. He is the proprietor of a rag and bottle warehouse near Lincoln's Inn, where he lives with his cat and drinks gin very heavily.

Krook is a dealer, who buys old pieces of furniture, books and papers, and his filthy shop is littered with parchment scrolls, dirty bottles and shabby, old books. Though he cannot read or write properly, he is aware that some of these papers may be valuable, and is keenly interested in all matters related to the High Court of Chancery and to the Jarndyce case. He is very secretive about his own affairs and so suspicious of others that he will not trust anyone to teach him to read and write.

He and his shop play an important part in *Bleak House*. Nemo, Miss Flite and Guppy's friend Jobling all have rooms in the warehouse at some stage in the novel, and both Lady Dedlock's letters to Captain Hawdon and the most recent Will in the Jarndyce case are found there by Grandfather Smallweed, who turns out to be Krook's brother-in-law.

But Krook's role seems to be more symbolic than realistic. He is known among his neighbours as the Lord Chancellor and his shop as the Court of Chancery, names which not only refer ironically to the hopeless muddle of the legal system proper, but which suggest that its confusions and injustices are to be found everywhere. The name Krook had clear associations with the world of deceit and trickery, even before the word acquired its modern meaning of a dishonest person, and Krook's death by spontaneous combustion in Chapter 33, 'the death of all Lord Chancellors in all Courts', can be interpreted as Dickens's way of symbolising the process by which he feels changes to the corrupt society of *Bleak House* may come. (A fuller account of Esther's visit to Krook's warehouse can be found in the next section.)

The Rouncewells

Mrs Rouncewell is the handsome old housekeeper at Chesney Wold, where she has been in service for fifty years. Her loyalty to the Dedlocks reveals another aspect of their characters, and her tale of the Ghost's Walk helps to create the atmosphere of impending disaster which threatens Lady Dedlock. Mrs Rouncewell's main role in the novel, however, is to contribute to the gallery of parent-child relationships.

Her elder son, after showing a good deal of mechanical ingenuity in his youth, became an extremely successful manufacturer and ironmaster. Though not ashamed of his mother's position, he is proud of his career as a prosperous industrialist, and provokes Sir Leicester by suggesting that his son Watt's fiancée Rosa needs a better education than that provided by the village school. He plays a prominent part in the election which defeats Sir Leicester later. Though Dickens is sympathetic to his spirit of independence and energy, as compared with Coodle and Doodle, he also points out how his industry is blighting the landscape.

Mrs Rouncewell's younger son, George, perhaps because he was her favourite, behaved wildly when young, and left home to join the army, where he became friendly with Captain Hawdon. A good-looking, brown-faced man of about fifty, he has the military bearing of an ex-trooper, and runs a shooting gallery near Leicester Square. His manly generosity is clearly displayed in his kindness to Phil Squod, Gridley and Jo. Because he is in debt to Grandfather Smallweed, he is forced to hand over an old letter from Hawdon to Tulkinghorn, and is wrongly arrested for Tulkinghorn's murder later. He refuses to hire a lawyer to defend himself, preferring to believe in simple assertions of his innocence. Indeed, he possesses a massive simplicity which is always impressive. George is deeply ashamed of the way he let his mother down by his bad behaviour, and tries to persuade his elder brother, the ironmaster, to remove him from her Will. The reconciliation of the two brothers is one of the most pleasant developments in the final stages of the novel, and George's return to Chesney Wold as Sir Leicester's manservant is a moving and dignified finale to his troubled career.

Watt, the ironmaster's son, falls in love with Rosa, Lady Dedlock's maid, and so accidentally causes the dispute between Sir Leicester and his father. Though almost certainly named after James Watt, the great inventor, his name also has associations with Watt Tyler, a leader in the Peasants' Revolt, and so reminds the reader of social as well as industrial revolutionaries.

Harold Skimpole
On first appearance, Harold Skimpole has an unusual but attractive personality. Despite a rather large head, his delicate face, sweet voice and vivacious manner make him very agreeable. A graceful and witty conversationalist, he is something of a gentleman-artist. Skilled at drawing, he is also fond of music, playing the piano, cello and flute.

The most striking aspect of Skimpole's personality, however, is his self-confessed lack of worldliness. He has no idea of time or money, he candidly confesses, and so is quite incapable of transacting any business. 'I am a mere child,' he frankly admits in Chapter 18, and has to rely on the help of friends such as Mr Jarndyce to look after him financially. Not surprisingly he frequently falls into debt, and has to be rescued by Richard and Esther early on in the novel, but later loses his furniture, and also gets into difficulties with a baker. All these experiences he handles with charm and cheerfulness.

While the reader may sympathise with Skimpole up to a point – after all, he might not be able to help being child-like – Esther begins to question his behaviour from very early on. She notices that he eats a basket of the finest peaches without a thought of paying for them, and she coolly records his views on the picturesque aspects of slavery. She wonders about the welfare of Mrs Skimpole and the children, and notes that he leaves them to deal with the angry baker whose chairs he borrowed and wore out.

Skimpole, in fact, is quite unfeeling about the Necketts, and cheerfully neglects his own family. A dabbler in art, he did compose half an opera once, we learn, but got tired of it. Significantly, he wins Sir Leicester's approval when he describes himself as 'a mere amateur' (Chapter 43), perhaps because his dilettantism, as compared with serious art, such as Dickens's, does not challenge Sir Leicester's aristocratic way of life.

Skimpole admits his irresponsibility quite openly to Esther in Chapter 37 when he says, 'I never was responsible in my life – I can't be.' But this kind of disavowal sounds less charming when it leads to the betrayal of Jo – and Skimpole a medical man! – and to a willingness to feed off Richard Carstone later.

Skimpole's description of Jarndyce as 'the Incarnation of Selfishness' (Chapter 61) is what we would expect of him by the end of the book, but Jarndyce's long-suffering toleration of him raises serious questions about Jarndyce's judgement.

The Smallweeds

The Smallweed family are among Dickens's finest examples of grotesque characters, for they are alternately comic and sinister, and sometimes both at the same time!

Joshua Smallweed, the grandfather, is a cantankerous, old money-grubber, often referred to as a spider or leech. Though so infirm he can only move from his porter's chair by his fireside when other people carry him, he is full of ferocious energy, frequently hurling a cushion at his elderly, deaf wife who sits the other side of the fire. He is obsessed with money and spends all his time scheming to get more. We may say of Joshua what Dickens says of Joshua's father, that 'The name of this old pagan's God [is] Compound Interest' (Chapter 21).

The twin grandchildren are equally mercenary. Fourteen-year-old Bartholomew and Judy are small for their ages – the name Smallweed suggests stunted growth, of course – and never enjoyed a proper childhood with toys and games, but share their grandfather's interest in money. Bart works in the same legal office as Mr Guppy, and Judy, though taught the trade of artificial-flower-making, looks after her grandfather's home in an unsavoury district called Mount Pleasant, where she bullies the young servant, Charley.

They threaten Trooper George, who owes them money, and virtually force him to hand over to Mr Tulkinghorn a letter he has from Captain Hawdon. When Krook dies, grandmother Smallweed proves to be his sister and inherits his property. Amongst it the Smallweeds find a bundle of letters Lady Dedlock wrote to her lover, which Inspector Bucket advises Sir Leicester to buy to protect his wife's reputation. The Smallweeds also find a new Will in the Jarndyce case, and give it to Mr Jarndyce in the hope of obtaining a large reward. Since that is to be based on the Will's value, however, the Smallweeds seem likely to be bitterly disappointed. As Detective Bucket says, 'there ain't one of the family that wouldn't sell the other for a pound or two, except the old lady – and she's only out of it because she's too weak in her mind to drive a bargain' (Chapter 62).

Mr and Mrs Snagsby

Mr and Mrs Snagsby have small but important parts in the plot of *Bleak House*, and also contribute to the variety of marriages which Dickens portrays in the novel.

Mr Snagsby has a small law-stationer's business in Cook's Court, near Chancery Lane, where he lives with his wife and their servant, Guster. He is a mild, balding man, with a scrub of black hair sticking out at the back, and timidly allows his wife, who is jealous and inquisitive by nature, to dominate their marriage.

Mr Snagsby employed Nemo as a law-writer and shows Tulkinghorn where he lodged in Krook's warehouse. He is present at Nemo's inquest, where he meets Jo, and when he later hears his story of the veiled lady, passes this information on to Tulkinghorn. Jo's interrogation by Tulkinghorn and Bucket disturbs Snagsby, however; he feels that he is party to a dangerous secret without knowing what it is, and begins to feel guilty. This increases his wife's suspicion of his behaviour, and she leaps to the conclusion that her husband is Jo's father! Her suspicions increase when Snagsby is also nearby at the time of Krook's mysterious death.

Mr Snagsby is really a tender-hearted man, however; he genuinely feels sorry for Jo, and is always giving him half-crowns. It is part of the comedy arising from his character that he never wants his wife to know about this. When Bucket's inquiries lead him to interrogate Guster in Chapter 59, the detective explains Mr Snagsby's behaviour to his wife, and reprimands her for her foolish jealousy. There are some signs that she will reform from now on.

Mr Vholes

Mr Vholes is a lawyer with minute and unwholesome chambers in Symond's Inn. Aged about fifty, he is a tall, thin man, with a rash on his face and thin lips. Normally dressed in black, and wearing black gloves, he has a remarkably lifeless manner.

Vholes becomes Richard's legal adviser in the Jarndyce case, and, though working assiduously on his behalf, gradually leads him further into debt. Although he claims to be open and truthful, and prides himself on always looking after Richard's interests, he encourages his hopes so that Richard sinks further and further into self-destruction. He tells Mr Jarndyce and Allan Woodcourt of Richard's money troubles, too, probably hoping that they will pay Richard's debts, though he knows that they disapprove of Richard's venture.

The name Vholes reminds the reader of the word for the mouse-like rodent, and Esther says 'there was something of the Vampire in him' (Chapter 60). Dickens compares him to various predatory animals, and describes him looking at Richard 'as if he were looking at his prey and charming it' in Chapter 37. Vholes taps his desk as if it were a coffin in Chapter 39, and his shadow is described as chilling the seed in the ground as it glided along in Chapter 45. Dickens sees Vholes as a blood-sucking creature, in other words, someone who feeds off others in order to keep himself alive.

Yet Vholes is also portrayed as someone who is concerned about the upbringing of his three daughters, and who supports his aged father in the Vale of Taunton. He is not necessarily to be regarded as a deliberately cruel person, therefore. Indeed he is very respectable. But he is a lawyer, and the one great principle of the English laws, Dickens says in Chapter 39, is 'to make business for itself', even if the results of doing so bring despair and destruction to Richard Carstone and many others. Mr Vholes is thus an unfeeling and irresponsible functionary of a legal system which *Bleak House* shows to be unjustly cruel and nightmarish. His efficiency as a servant of that system raises many disturbing questions.

5 SPECIMEN PASSAGE AND COMMENTARY

5.1 SUMMARY

Esther Summerson has just been appointed companion to Ada Clare, a young ward of the Court of Chancery, with her cousin Richard, and is travelling with them to her employer's house in St. Albans. On the way they spend the night at Mrs Jellyby's in London and, going for a walk the next morning (in Chapter 5) they meet Miss Flite, whom they had already met in Court the day before. She insists on inviting them to her lodgings:

She had stopped at a shop, over which was written KROOK, RAG AND BOTTLE WAREHOUSE. Also, in long thin letters, KROOK, DEALER IN MARINE STORES. In one part of the window was a picture of a red paper mill, at which a cart was unloading a quantity of sacks of old rags. In another, was the inscription, BONES BOUGHT. In another, KITCHEN-STUFF BOUGHT. In another, OLD IRON BOUGHT. In another, WASTE PAPER BOUGHT. In another, LADIES' AND GENTLEMEN'S WARDROBES BOUGHT. Everything seemed to be bought and nothing to be sold there. In all parts of the window were quantities of dirty bottles: blacking bottles, medicine bottles, ginger-beer and soda-water bottles, pickle bottles, wine bottles, ink bottles: I am reminded by mentioning the latter, that the shop had, in several little particulars, the air of being in a legal neighbourhood, and of being, as it were, a dirty hanger-on and disowned relation of the law. There were a great many ink bottles. There was a little tottering bench of shabby old volumes, outside the door, labelled 'Law Books, all at 9d.' Some of the inscriptions I have enumerated were written in law-hand, like the papers I had seen in Kenge and Carboy's office, and the letters I had so long received from the firm. Among them was one, in the same writing, having nothing to do with the business of the shop, but announcing that a respectable man aged forty-five wanted engrossing or copying to execute with neatness and despatch: Address to Nemo, care of Mr. Krook within. There were several second-hand bags, blue and red, hanging up. A little way within the shop-door, lay heaps of old crackled parchment scrolls, and discoloured and dog's-eared law-papers. I could have fancied that all the rusty keys, of which there must have been hundreds huddled together as old iron, had once belonged to doors of rooms or strong chests in lawyers' offices. The litter of rags tumbled partly into and partly out of a one-legged wooden scale, hanging without any counterpoise from a beam, might have been counsellors' bands and gowns torn up. One had only to fancy, as Richard whispered to Ada and me while we all stood looking in, that yonder bones in a corner, piled together and picked very clean, were the bones of clients, to make the picture complete.

As it was still foggy and dark, and as the shop was blinded besides by the wall of Lincoln's Inn, intercepting the light within a couple of yards, we should not have seen so much but for a lighted lantern that an old man in spectacles and a hairy cap was carrying about in the shop. Turning towards the door, he now caught sight of us. He was short, cadaverous, and withered; with his head sunk sideways between his shoulders, and the breath issuing in visible smoke from his mouth, as if he were on fire within. His throat, chin, and eyebrows were so frosted with white hairs, and so gnarled with veins and puckered skin, that he looked, from his breast upward, like some old root in a fall of snow.

'Hi hi!' said the old man coming to the door. 'Have you anything to sell?'

We naturally drew back and glanced at our conductress, who had been trying to open the house-door with a key she had taken from her pocket, and to whom Richard now said that, as we had had the pleasure of seeing where she lived, we would leave her, being pressed for time. But she was not to be so easily left. She became so fantastically and pressingly earnest in her entreaties that we would walk up, and see her apartment for an instant; and was so bent, in her harmless way, on leading me in, as part of the good omen she desired; that I (whatever the others might do) saw nothing for it but to comply. I suppose we were all more or less curious, – at any rate, when the old man added his persuasions to hers, and said, 'Aye, aye! Please her! It won't take a minute! Come in, come in! Come in through the shop, if t'other door's out of order!' we all went in, stimulated by Richard's laughing encouragement, and relying on his protection.

'My landlord, Krook,' said the little old lady, condescending to him from her lofty station, as she presented him to us. 'He is called among the neighbours the Lord Chancellor. His shop is called the Court of Chancery. He is a very eccentric person. He is very odd. Oh, I assure you he is very odd!'

She shook her head a great many times, and tapped her forehead with her finger, to express to us that we must have the goodness to excuse him, 'For he is a little - you know! - M - !' said the little old lady, with great stateliness. The old man overheard, and laughed.

'It's true enough,' he said, going before us with the lantern, 'that they call me the Lord Chancellor, and call my shop Chancery. And why do you think they call me the Lord Chancellor, and my shop Chancery?'

'I don't know, I am sure!' said Richard, rather carelessly.

'You see,' said the old man, stopping and turning round, 'they - Hi! Here's lovely hair! I have got three sacks of ladies' hair below, but none so beautiful and fine as this. What colour, and what texture!'

'That'll do, my good friend!' said Richard, strongly disapproving of his having drawn one of Ada's tresses through his yellow hand. 'You can admire as the rest of us do, without taking that liberty.'

The old man darted at him a sudden look, which even called my attention from Ada, who, startled and blushing, was so remarkably beautiful that she seemed to fix the wandering attention of the little old lady herself. But as Ada interposed, and laughingly said she could only feel proud of such genuine admiration, Mr Krook shrunk into his former self as suddenly as he had leaped out of it.

'You see I have so many things here,' he resumed, holding up the lantern, 'of so many kinds, and all, as the neighbours think (but *they* know nothing), wasting away and going to rack and ruin, that that's why they have given me and my place a christening. And I have so many parchmentses and papers in my stock. And I have a liking for rust and must and cobwebs. And all's fish that comes to my net. And I can't abear to part with anything I once lay hold of (or so my neighbours think, but what do *they* know?) or to alter anything, or to have any sweeping, nor scouring, nor cleaning, nor repairing going on about me. That's the way I've got the ill name of Chancery. I don't mind. I go to see my noble and learned brother pretty well every day, when he sits in the Inn. He don't notice me, but I notice him. There's no great odds betwixt us. We both grub on in a muddle. Hi, Lady Jane!'

A large grey cat leaped from some neighbouring shelf on his shoulder, and startled us all.

'Hi! show 'em how you scratch. Hi! Tear, my lady!' said her master.

The cat leaped down, and ripped at a bundle of rags with her tigerish claws, with a sound that it set my teeth on edge to hear.

'She'd do as much for anyone I was to set her on,' said the old man. 'I deal in cat-skins among other general matters, and hers was offered to me. It's a very fine skin, as you may see, but I didn't have it stripped off. *That* warn't like Chancery practice though, says you!'

5.2 CRITICAL COMMENTARY

The first point to remember about this passage is that the narrator is Esther Summerson, the intelligent young woman who is to become one of the central figures in *Bleak House*. Because of her illegitimate birth and repressive upbringing, Esther is very unsure of herself, and though extremely observant, very reluctant to make judgements. She tends at this stage in the novel to record what she sees, and leave the reader to make up his or her mind about what she is describing, though her caring attitude towards Mrs Jellyby's children, and her attempts to bring order to that chaotic household have shown the reader how responsible Esther is.

Miss Flite, the 'she' of the first paragraph, has already been introduced in Chapter 3 as an eccentric old lady, who regularly attends the Court of Chancery in the hope of receiving a favourable judgement, and her rambling conversation has already led Richard to brand her a 'Mad'. It is part of her friendly but peculiar behaviour that she has insisted in inviting Esther, Richard and Ada to her lodgings, where they now arrive.

Krook's rag and bottle warehouse, where she has rooms, is a large shop, and its owner evidently buys materials, such as bottles, old rags and paper, which other people have already discarded. The repetition of four sentences beginning with the phrase 'In another' rhetorically emphasises the great quantity of goods purchased, and the owner Krook is thus revealed as very acquisitive, but because 'Everything seemed to be bought, and nothing to be sold there', and what is bought is already soiled, the shop is littered with refuse, and is dirty and untidy. The bench holding shabby old books is 'tottering', and the floor is covered with 'crackled' parchments, 'discoloured' law-papers and rusty keys.

The picture of decay and disorder is more than that, however. The description of the fog in the Court of Chancery in the first chapter of *Bleak House*, the melancholy weather at Chesney Wold in the second, and Mrs Jellyby's unruly and smoky household in Chapter 4 all employ similar references to dirt and fog in ways which link these images to the human irresponsibility and selfishness of the people who live and work in those places. The filth and squalor of Krook's warehouse, then, expresses something of Krook's own diseased and uncaring personality, and it is significant that keys, which are to become symbols of Esther's responsible housekeeping in the very next chapter, have here been allowed by Krook to become 'rusty'.

More than that, however, this first paragraph also associates many of the examples of dirt and decay specifically with the law. The shop is in 'a legal neighbourhood' as if it were a 'disowned relation of the law', Esther says, and so it is not surprising to find so many legal objects here, but they are all 'shabby,' 'crackled,' 'discoloured' and 'dog's-eared,' suggesting that the law itself is worn out, too. The wooden scale, which might remind the reader of the scales of even-handed justice, is broken, we notice, and weighed down by what look like lawyers' torn gowns, as if it is lawyers who prevent justice being fair, in other words.

The presence of so much paper, waste paper, old law books and parchment scrolls, all perfectly realistic in the context of Krook's shop, also draws attention to the importance of papers, letters and legal documents in the novel. The Jarndyce case involves a disputed Will, and Lady Dedlock is startled by some familiar handwriting in Chapter 2. Mrs Jellyby's house is strewn with philanthropic letters in Chapter 4 and now Krook's shop is full of paper, too. *Bleak House* is a novel in which documents play a very important part, with disputes over Wills and missing letters at the heart of it, and the presence of so much paper in Krook's shop emphasises the importance of documents. Some critics have even compared the events in *Bleak House* to a series of documents which invite the reader's interpretation, as the characters in the novel itself have to read and understand documents, and learn to interpret each other's behaviour correctly.

With a terrible irony, in view of what is to happen to him later, Richard notices some old bones in a corner of the shop, and jokes that they look like the bones of a dead client; and one final irony of this richly evocative paragraph is Esther's observation, among all the legal papers, of a man's advertising for work engrossing or transcribing legal documents. That man is Nemo, later discovered to be Esther's father, and, since he lodges at Krook's house, Esther might well have accidentally met him on this visit. The fact that Esther recognises the hand-writing further suggests that Nemo himself may have been the very person who wrote to Esther from Kenge and Carboy's, including, for example, the letter Esther quotes in Chapter 3.

The second paragraph of this passage continues to use the imagery of darkness and dirt associated with the theme of irresponsibility, and the reader is reminded that it is still foggy in the early morning, and that Krook's shop is also 'blinded' by a wall which prevents much daylight getting in. The fact that it is a wall of Lincoln's Inn and that the word 'blinded' is used (rather than a more neutral work such as 'hidden') suggests that the law itself inflicts damage by keeping out the light. An old man now enters, aged seventy-six, we learn later in the novel, whose appearance confirms the impression of decay and death suggested by his shop. He is, in fact, described in terms of a decay so wintry that he seems barely alive, for he is 'withered' with age, has 'frosted' hair, and looks like 'an old root'. The adjective 'cadaverous', meaning corpse-like, clinches the picture of his deathly appearance, and the description of his breath as 'smoke', which connects up with the references to fog and smoke in earlier chapters, is a terrible anticipation of his death later in the novel.

Yet the old man is not quite dead, for he still has one overwhelming interest in life, and without concerning himself with morning greetings or expressions of pleasure, he reveals his materialistic and acquisitive philosophy with the words, 'Have you anything to sell?' The cash-nexus dominates his life.

Miss Flite's introduction of the old man in the fifth paragraph is truly devastating, for she reveals that this barely-living figure of death, this owner of an appalling warehouse cluttered with filth and litter, is known among his neighbours as the Lord Chancellor, and his shop is called the Court of Chancery. Dickens's symbolism has now become quite explicit. The reader is no longer following a story about a group of individual characters from which he may infer a general or thematic meaning; for the novelist, via Esther's narrative, is likening the High Court of Chancery and the office of the Lord Chancellor, two of Britain's noblest representations of justice and order, to this mercenary old man and his filthy shop. Krook's name, even before it acquired its modern meaning of a dishonest person, already had associations with the world of deceit and trickery, so Dickens is clearly telling the reader more about his character by giving him that name, and Miss Flite adds to the horrifying impression the reader develops of his character and the law when she says that Krook is 'very odd' and 'a little - you know - M - !' She presumably means Mad.

This nightmarish picture is now intensified by a curious but frightening hiatus. After proudly admitting that he is known as the Lord Chancellor, Krook is about to tell his visitors the reason, when he suddenly notices Ada's rich, golden hair. It was quite common in the nineteenth century for young women to sell their hair to be made into wigs, and Krook has evidently already bought some for that purpose, but in talking of the 'three sacks of ladies' hair below' and drawing his 'yellow hand' through Ada's hair, the withered old man suddenly behaves like an evil magician in an old folk-tale, about to do an innocent young girl terrible harm. Krook and his shop are transformed into an evil magician in a loathsome lair. Yet this is the man popularly known as the Lord Chancellor! What does this reference tell the reader of the real Lord Chancellor?

Richard's protective intervention on Ada's behalf is surely an anticipation of the loving relationship which is to grow up between them later, and, though Krook looks daggers at the young man, Ada's laughing response calms the situation. The way Krook is said to shrink back into his 'former self' heightens the impression of his macabre evil, however.

Krook now proceeds to elaborate on why he is known as the Lord Chancellor: he possesses many things which are wasting away; he has many old documents; and he is very fond of dust and cobwebs. He offers, in other words, an appalling picture of that court which was supposed to offer justice to all, especially the less fortunate members of society. He is acquisitive like Chancery, and so cannot part with anything, as Chancery is unable to let go of Jarndyce or Miss Flite or Gridley or subsequently Richard. He cannot bear alterations (or improvements?), and he abhors sweeping, scouring or cleaning, the characteristics of so many irresponsible people in the novel, as compared with Esther and the Bagnets, for example, whose energy and responsibility are symbolised by their household skills.

The portrait of Krook, in other words, with all his filth and waste and irresponsibility, enlarges the reader's consciousness of the law in *Bleak House*, to emphasise its waste and irresponsibility. When Krook says, 'We both grub on in a muddle', Dickens is saying by analogy that the court established to protect the poor is also dirty, inefficient, money-grubbing and chaotic.

But, though Krook amplifies the reader's understanding of the law and Chancery, he also exists as a character in his own right. We have already noticed his mercenary qualities – 'Have you anything to sell?' – and in the same paragraph as Krook says 'There's no great odds betwixt us', we learn that he attends the Court of Chancery every day, as Miss Flite does, and as Richard is to do also before the novel ends. We also gather that he is an embittered person who despises his neighbours – 'what do *they* know?' – and later learn that he is so suspicious that, though he cannot read or write himself, he will not trust anyone else to teach him, in case they teach him wrongly!

Krook exists, in other words, not just as a symbol of the court's evil, but as a sign that its irresponsibility and selfishness are everywhere, even among the bourgeois, shopkeeping classes. The novel has already shown us decay in Chancery, lassitude at Chesney Wold, stern repression in Esther's upbringing, and child neglect at the Jellyby's. Now Dickens shows us the same unfeeling irresponsibility, though in a more macabre form, through the picture of Krook and his shop.

Though Krook despises his neighbours, he evidently does enjoy the company of a large, grey cat and this now leaps down from a shelf and startles everyone, the presence of the cat reinforcing the impression Krook gave earlier of a supernatural demon by the association of cats with witchcraft. This cat is called 'Lady Jane', the name reminding the reader of the young queen who died young accused of treason, and she is no warm, reassuring companion for Krook's old age, but a ferocious animal 'with tigerish claws' that Krook keeps as a kind of watch-guard. In a story where birds are frequently used almost as symbols of innocence – one thinks of Boythorn's canary or the larks and linnets Miss Flite keeps upstairs – Lady Jane is a threatening predator, to be associated with such human predators as Tulkinghorn and Vholes, and, by association now, with Krook himself. Krook values the cat so much, in fact, that he decided not to have her killed so that her skin and fur should be stripped off and sold, an act, he adds with savage irony, which the Court of Chancery practises with its legal clients.

Dickens's account of Esther's first visit to Krook's shop is important, not only because it offers a perspective on the Court of Chancery, by comparing Krook's shop with the court, but because it throws light on the world beyond. The shop has its tentacles everywhere. Krook, Miss Flite and Nemo live there, and Jobling comes to lodge there later. Captain Hawdon's letters from Lady Dedlock are found there, and the Smallweeds discover the most valid Will in the Jarndyce case there.

It is there, of course, that Krook is found dead of spontaneous combustion in Chapter 32, an incident some readers criticise as far-fetched and implausible. But Krook's presentation throughout the novel is an extraordinary mixture of realism and symbolism, his function being to suggest not only the monstrous inequities of Chancery and the legal system but also the seedy world of dishonest dealers and shady businesses. His death is thus properly associated not only with the dirt, old papers and rags of his sordid premises, but also symbolises the ultimately self-destructive culmination of all the forces of greed and irresponsibility in the novel. Though Dickens was not a revolutionary, the awesome symbolism of Krook's death by spontaneous combustion is an expression of revolutionary power by a dramatic genius, suggesting not merely that Krook dies, but that he dies 'the death of all Chancellors in all Courts'.

6 CRITICAL RECEPTION

Bleak House was a great popular success with the reading public from its first appearance in monthly parts from March 1852 until its triumphal conclusion in September 1853. Sales of the first episode exceeded 38 000 and settled down to about 34 000 per month thereafter. Remarking on its enormous sales, compared with those of its very popular predecessor *David Copperfield*, Dickens talked of its 'beating dear old Copperfield by a round ten thousand or more,' and added, 'I have never had so many readers.' The novel's success in America was even greater, for when the story was serialised in *Harper's* magazine, 118 000 copies were sold each month, and it has been calculated that no fewer than 250 000 copies were supplied to American readers by 1853. Though it is difficult to estimate the size of the first book edition in Britain, as the publishers included it with the size of the sales of the monthly parts, it is safe to say that *Bleak House* was one of the greatest successes of Dickens's amazingly successful career.

Many of the literary critics also praised the novel enthusiastically. *Bentley's Monthly Review* (October 1853) regarded it as 'the greatest, the least faulty, the most beautiful of all the works which the pen of Dickens has given to the world', and particularly praised the portraits of Esther and Lady Dedlock. *Putnam's Magazine* (November 1853) was equally enthusiastic about Boythorn and Skimpole, Turveydrop and Chadband, and, though the *Athenaeum* (September 1853) had reservations about Esther, it gave generous praise to the handling of Lady Dedlock's history and to Mr Bucket. 'In his own particular walk,' the magazine sums up, 'Dickens has rarely, if ever, been happier than in *Bleak House*.'

What Dickens's contemporary reviewers valued above all, it is clear, was the strength and variety of his powers of characterisation, even when those reviewers did not always agree about the success of individual creations. There was very little attempt to consider the deeper purposes of *Bleak House*, though *Bentley's Monthly Review* had some doubts about the effectiveness of attacking Chancery, and the subtler instruments of Dickens's story-telling, such as his symbolism or use of *déjà vu* effects, are similarly ignored.

The aspect of Dickens's art that most worried critics was his construction of plot, and reservations about this element of *Bleak House* accounts for the mixed nature of a number of contemporary reviews which otherwise praised the novel warmly. Thus the *Illustrated London News*, the *Spectator* (both September 1853) and *Bentley's Miscellany* (October 1853), while praising *Bleak House* in general, cannot forbear criticising the novel's construction, for being contrived and artificial, for not connecting the Chancery case with the Dedlocks, or for introducing characters such as Skimpole who were thought to be irrelevant to the plot. Even these readers who failed to see the carefully-wrought thematic unity of the novel, however, usually considered that its merits, the characterisation, the feeling, the power of satire and the presence of so many brilliant episodes more than compensated for weaknesses, a view summed up by the *Westminster Review* (October 1853) which said 'They who find fault with *Bleak House*, and they must be many, can only quarrel with it as with what they love.'

A few readers were more hostile, however. *The Rambler*, a Roman Catholic journal, as well as attacking *Bleak House* for what it regarded as superficial characterisation and a want of wit, was particularly offended by Dickens's being 'ignorant of the very elements of a religious faith', and regarded his portrait of the Chadbands as 'perfect failures'. *The Eclectic Review* (December 1853) was also annoyed by the portrait of the Chadbands, and argued that the portraits of Mrs Jellyby and Mrs Pardiggle held up to ridicule the aims of the missionary and benevolent institutions they served. *Blackwood's Edinburgh Magazine* (April 1855) was similarly worried by Dickens's attack on nonconformist religion, through the comic figure of Chadband.

Though we may regard these unfriendly reviews as the products of special interests, rather like G. H. Lewes's criticism of spontaneous combustion for being unscientific (*Leader*, December 1852) or J. S. Mill's dismissal of *Bleak House* (in a letter of March 1854) because he thought it ridiculed the rights of women, the novel did, in fact, soon come to lose the warm praise with which it had been initially greeted. By the late 1850s and early 1860s, Dickens's whole reputation came under review, and his later novels were often severely criticised, *Bleak House* being linked with *Little Dorrit* (1857) and *A Tale of Two Cities* (1859) as examples of the deterioration of his art – 'bad, melodramatic, pretentious, and, above all, dull', as the *Saturday Review* called them in February 1861. *The Times* reviewers ignored many of Dickens's later works, and the *Westminster Review* confidently said in 1864 that 'We cannot think that he will live as an English classic.' Even as perceptive a critic as the young Henry James came to say that '*Bleak House* was forced', and that Dickens was only 'the greatest of superficial novelists' (*The Nation*, December 1865).

The reasons for this change in critical attitudes towards Dickens are many and complicated. The emergence of William Makepeace Thackeray, in particular, and later the Brontës and George Eliot, had given Dickens a number of novel-writing rivals whose work could be compared with his, sometimes to Dickens's disadvantage, especially in terms of realism and plot-construction as the Victorians perceived them. Secondly, the nature of Dickens's work did begin to change in the 1850s, from the time of *Bleak House* especially, and Dickens's increasing seriousness did disappoint many readers who had enjoyed the humour and exuberance of his earlier books.

Walter Bagehot's long review-article on 'Charles Dickens' for the *National Review* (October 1858) is a very clear expression of the anxieties of many Victorian readers about Dickens's work, with its worries about the peculiarities of his prose-style, his clumsy plots, the love-elements, the use of pathos, and what Bagehot terms Dickens's 'sentimental radicalism'. Anthony Trollope was even more cutting in his *Autobiography* of 1883, criticising his characters because 'they are not human, nor are any of the characters human which Dickens has portrayed', while of Dickens's style he said 'it is impossible to speak in praise'. The writer and editor Leslie Stephen probably summed up what many late Victorians thought of Dickens when in 1888 he made his famous barbed remark: 'If literary fame could be safely measured by popularity with the half-educated, Dickens must claim the highest position among English novelists.'

Despite this fall in critical esteem, however, the popular appeal of Dickens's books with the common reader continued unabated. Twelve years after his death in 1870 no fewer than 4 239 000 copies of his books had been sold in England alone, while between 1900 and 1906 his publishers, Chapman and Hall, sold over two million copies.

The first signs of a critical revaluation of Dickens began to appear in the last years of the nineteenth century, with George Gissing's *Charles Dickens: a Critical Study* in 1898, and G. K. Chesterton helped to produce the first of several books he wrote about Dickens in 1903. Substantial rehabilitation of Dickens as a major, almost Shakespearian figure really began about the 1940s, with George Orwell's essay 'Charles Dickens', which appeared in 1939, and Edmund Wilson's influential article 'Dickens: the Two Scrooges', in 1941, the same year as Humphrey House's thoughtful book, *The Dickens World*.

The reputation of *Bleak House* has continued to rise, too, so that it now stands near the peak of Dickens's whole achievement. Two books on *Bleak House* between them contain some of the best essays on the novel.

Twentieth Century Interpretions of 'Bleak House, (Prentice-Hall: New Jersey, 1968) edited by Jacob Korg, contains work by such scholars as Edgar Johnson, Robert A. Donovan and J. Hillis Miller, while A. E. Dyson's *Bleak House: a Casebook* (Macmillan, 1969) contains useful material by Victorian reviewers and contemporary material by such critics as C. B. Cox, W. J. Harvey and the editor himself.

Bleak House has, in fact, become one of the most widely discussed and widely praised of all Dickens's novels. *The New Cambridge Bibliography of English Literature*, edited by George Watson in 1969, for example, lists over forty articles about it, compared with thirty-four about the immensely popular *David Copperfield*, and twenty for *Hard Times*, the works which preceded and succeeded it.

Critical discussion of the novel tends to concentrate on four areas which Dickens's Victorian readers perhaps underestimated or misunderstood. Writers such as R. A. Donovan and J. Hillis Miller have shown that while the artistic centre of the novel seems to be Chancery and a satirical attack on the law, those particular targets of Dickens's satire are in fact part of a wider moral and social analysis, so that other, apparently unrelated parts of the novel, such as the story of the Dedlocks or the neglect of Mrs Jellyby's children, also belong to a more coherent and organic structure than Victorian readers perceived. Other critics have reinforced this point by drawing attention to Dickens's magnificent control over the apparently heterogeneous mixture of ingredients in *Bleak House*, and Norman Friedman's study of the novel's symbolism together with W. J. Harvey's examination of the roles of the two narrators show just how intricately and skilfully the whole work is articulated.

Another important emphasis in recent interpretations of the novel is the high praise given to Dickens's psychological insights. Dickens's characters have often been praised for their possession of admired virtues or their entertainment value, but many modern readers also praise them for their inner truthfulness, whether they are depicted in Dickens's realistic or his symbolical style. Thus William Axton and Q. D. Leavis both praise Dickens for the authenticity of his portrait of the emotionally crippled Esther, while Arnold Kettle praises him for the symbolic truth of Krook's presentation.

Finally, most critics today interpret novels as imaginative and autonomous works of art, rather than photographic documents, and they accept Dickens's unique mixture of realism and melodrama, symbolism and comedy, because of the profound truths he conveys rather than because of the way he painstakingly creates the illusion of everyday reality. In this sense his novels may be said to be about living, even when they are not particularly life-like.

Many readers agree with Edmund Wilson's view that in the way Dickens wrote a detective story which is also a social and moral fable, he was able to combine the skills of a popular entertainer with the insights of a great and serious artist in a manner for which the most appropriate term is Shakespearian.

REVISION QUESTIONS

1. Is there any unifying theme in *Bleak House* or does it consist of a series of brilliant but unrelated episodes?
2. 'Far from being a sentimental good angel, Esther has a perfect psychological consistency.' How far do you agree with this statement?
3. Examine the part played by coincidence in *Bleak House*.
4. How helpful do you find Edmund Wilson's comment that '*Bleak House* is a detective story which is also a social fable'?
5. Discuss the symbolism of *Bleak House*.
6. Examine the parts played in *Bleak House* by (a) the Smallweeds, and (b) the Bagnets.
7. Why do you think that Dickens used a double narrative technique in *Bleak House*, and how successfully do you think he employed it?
8. 'The Lady Dedlock plot is weak in itself and not connected with the rest of *Bleak House*.' Discuss.
9. Discuss the part played by the law and lawyers in *Bleak House*.
10. Discuss Dickens's treatment of parent-child relationships in *Bleak House* and examine how far they are related to the other concerns of the novel.
11. 'In *Bleak House*, I have purposely dwelt upon the romantic side of familiar things.' How effectively do you think Dickens achieved his intention?
12. Examine the significance of papers, letters and legal documents in *Bleak House*.

FURTHER READING

There are many different editions of the novel, but two recent ones which may be particularly recommended are the Norton Critical Edition of *Bleak House*, edited by George Ford and Sylvère Monod (Norton: New York, 1977), and the Penguin English Library Edition of *Bleak House*, edited by Norman Page, with an Introduction by J. Hillis Miller (Penguin, 1971).

Biography

Forster, John, *The Life of Charles Dickens*, revised with new material by A. J. Hoppé, 2 vols (Dent, 1966). This is an important account by one of Dickens's closest friends, and the best biography.

Johnson, Edgar, *Charles Dickens: His Tragedy and Triumph* (revised edn, Penguin, 1979). The standard modern biography, containing much new information.

Fielding, K. J., *Charles Dickens: a Critical Introduction* (2nd edn, enlarged, Longman, 1965). A short and useful introduction to Dickens's life and work.

Background

Collins, P., *Dickens and Crime* (Macmillan, 1962). Particularly interesting on Dickens's treatment of criminals and the police.

Cruikshank, R. J., *Charles Dickens and Early Victorian England* (Pitman, 1949). A most readable and illustrated survey of the period.

House, H., *The Dickens World*, revised edn (OUP, 1942). A stimulating work, dealing with Dickens's attitude towards such topics as benevolence, politics and religion.

Young, G. M., *Victorian England: Portrait of an Age*, 2nd edn (OUP, 1964). A brief but concentrated historical survey.

Criticism

Axton, William, 'The Trouble with Esther', *Modern Languages Quarterly*, vol, 26, 1965. A skilful attempt to explain Esther's complicated personality.

Butt, J. and Tillotson, K., *Dickens at Work* (Methuen, 1957). Particularly good on the topical references in *Bleak House*.

Dyson, A. E. (ed.), *Dickens: Bleak House: a Casebook* (Macmillan, 1969). As well as some contemporary documents about the working class and about sanitary conditions in the nineteenth century, this collection also contains essays by such critics as J. Hillis Miller, W. J. Harvey and the editor himself.

Friedman, Norman, 'The Shadow and the Sun: Notes towards a Reading of *Bleak House*', Boston University *Studies in English*, vol. 33, 1957. An early study of the symbolism of *Bleak House*.

Kettle, A., 'Dickens and the Popular Tradition', *The Carleton Miscellany*, vol. 3, 1961. Especially interesting on Dickens's presentation of Krook.

Korg, Jacob (ed.), *Twentieth Century Interpretations of 'Bleak House': a Collection of Critical Essays* (Prentice-Hall: New Jersey, 1968). Another stimulating collection including Robert A. Donovan's essay on 'Structure and Idea in *Bleak House*'.

Leavis, F. R. and Q. D., *Dickens and Novelist* (Chatto & Windus, 1970). Chapter 3 of this important but difficult book contains a brilliant account of *Bleak House*.

Miller, J. Hillis, *Charles Dickens: the World of his Novels* (OUP, 1958).

Nabokov, V., *Lectures in Literature*, ed. Fredson Bowers, introduction by John Updike (Weidenfeld & Nicolson, 1980). This contains a most stimulating lecture on *Bleak House*.

Newsom, Robert, *'Bleak House' and the Novel Tradition* (Columbia University Press: New York, 1977). An interesting attempt to show how Dickens's narrative art in *Bleak House* reveals the tension implicit in all fiction.

THE MACMILLAN SHAKESPEARE

General Editor: PETER HOLLINDALE
Advisory Editor: PHILIP BROCKBANK

The Macmillan Shakespeare features:
* clear and uncluttered texts with modernised punctuation and spelling wherever possible;
* full explanatory notes printed on the page facing the relevant text for ease of reference;
* stimulating introductions which concentrate on content, dramatic effect, character and imagery, rather than mere dates and sources.

Above all, The Macmillan Shakespeare treats each play as a work for the theatre which can also be enjoyed on the page.

CORIOLANUS
Editor: Tony Parr

THE WINTER'S TALE
Editor: Christopher Parry

MUCH ADO ABOUT NOTHING
Editor: Jan McKeith

RICHARD II
Editor: Richard Adams

RICHARD III
Editor: Richard Adams

HENRY IV, PART I
Editor: Peter Hollindale

HENRY IV, PART II
Editor: Tony Parr

HENRY V
Editor: Brian Phythian

AS YOU LIKE IT
Editor: Peter Hollindale

A MIDSUMMER NIGHT'S DREAM
Editor: Norman Sanders

THE MERCHANT OF VENICE
Editor: Christopher Parry

THE TAMING OF THE SHREW
Editor: Robin Hood

TWELFTH NIGHT
Editor: E. A. J. Honigmann

THE TEMPEST
Editor: A. C. Spearing

ROMEO AND JULIET
Editor: James Gibson

JULIUS CAESAR
Editor: D. R. Elloway

MACBETH
Editor: D. R. Elloway

HAMLET
Editor: Nigel Alexander

ANTONY AND CLEOPATRA
Editors: Jan McKeith and
Richard Adams

OTHELLO
Editors: Celia Hilton and R. T. Jones

KING LEAR
Editor: Philip Edwards

MACMILLAN STUDENTS' NOVELS

General Editor: JAMES GIBSON

The Macmillan Students' Novels are low-priced, new editions of major classics, aimed at the first examination candidate. Each volume contains:

* enough explanation and background material to make the novels accessible – and rewarding to pupils with little or no previous knowledge of the author or the literary period;

* detailed notes elucidate matters of vocabulary, interpretation and historical background;

* eight pages of plates comprising facsimiles of manuscripts and early editions, portraits of the author and photographs of the geographical setting of the novels.

JANE AUSTEN: MANSFIELD PARK
Editor: Richard Wirdnam

JANE AUSTEN: NORTHANGER ABBEY
Editor: Raymond Wilson

JANE AUSTEN: PRIDE AND PREJUDICE
Editor: Raymond Wilson

JANE AUSTEN: SENSE AND SENSIBILITY
Editor: Raymond Wilson

JANE AUSTEN: PERSUASION
Editor: Richard Wirdnam

CHARLOTTE BRONTË: JANE EYRE
Editor: F. B. Pinion

EMILY BRONTË: WUTHERING HEIGHTS
Editor: Graham Handley

JOSEPH CONRAD: LORD JIM
Editor: Peter Hollindale

CHARLES DICKENS: GREAT EXPECTATIONS
Editor: James Gibson

CHARLES DICKENS: HARD TIMES
Editor: James Gibson

CHARLES DICKENS: OLIVER TWIST
Editor: Guy Williams

CHARLES DICKENS: A TALE OF TWO CITIES
Editor: James Gibson

GEORGE ELIOT: SILAS MARNER
Editor: Norman Howlings

GEORGE ELIOT: THE MILL ON THE FLOSS
Editor: Graham Handley

D. H. LAWRENCE: SONS AND LOVERS
Editor: James Gibson

D. H. LAWRENCE: THE RAINBOW
Editor: James Gibson

MARK TWAIN: HUCKLEBERRY FINN
Editor: Christopher Parry

Mastering English Literature
Richard Gill

Mastering English Literature will help readers both to enjoy English Literature and to be successful in 'O' levels, 'A' levels and other public exams. It is an introduction to the study of poetry, novels and drama which helps the reader in four ways – by providing ways of approaching literature, by giving examples and practice exercises, by offering hints on how to write about literature, and by the author's own evident enthusiasm for the subject. With extracts from more than 200 texts, this is an enjoyable account of how to get the maximum satisfaction out of reading, whether it be for formal examinations or simply for pleasure.

Work Out English Literature ('A' level)
S.H. Burton

This book familiarises 'A' level English Literature candidates with every kind of test which they are likely to encounter. Suggested answers are worked out step by step and accompanied by full author's commentary. The book helps students to clarify their aims and establish techniques and standards so that they can make appropriate responses to similar questions when the examination pressures are on. It opens up fresh ways of looking at the full range of set texts, authors and critical judgements and motivates students to know more of these matters.

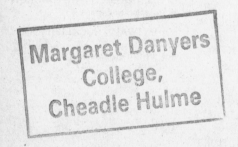